Activities for
an Interactive Classroom

Activities for
an Interactive Classroom

Jeffrey N. Golub
University of South Florida

National Council of Teachers of English
1111 W. Kenyon Road, Urbana, Illinois 61801-1096

NCTE Editorial Board: Hazel Davis, Keith Gilyard, Ronald Jobe, Joyce Kinkead, Louise W. Phelps, Charles Suhor, Chair, ex officio, Michael Spooner, ex officio

Manuscript Editor: Robert A. Heister/Humanities & Sciences Associates

Production Editor: Michael G. Ryan

Interior Design: Doug Burnett

Cover Design: Doug Burnett

NCTE Stock Number: 00465–3050

Library of Congress Cataloging-in-Publication Data

Golub, Jeffrey N., 1944–
    Activities for an interactive classroom / Jeffrey N. Golub.
       p.   cm.
    Includes bibliographical references.
    ISBN 0-8141-0046-5
    1. English language—Study and teaching (Secondary) 2. English language—Rhetoric—Study and teaching. 3. Active learning.
    I. Title.
    LB1613.G62 1994
    428′.0071′2—dc20   94-22134
                                                    CIP

For
Roy Alin—
my teacher, my friend

Contents

Foreword

When asked or required to change their accustomed practices and beliefs, even for what seems a brilliant educational innovation or transformation, why do so many teachers refuse? The profession could profit from a sweeping and statistically scrupulous poll to confirm what many of us have long suspected: teachers often have solid and compelling reasons for their refusal.

Many teachers today could only be characterized as change-shocked. They have been asked to change their teaching practices so often for the Curricular Fad of the Week that some have become numb or incapable—I mean literally—of yet another shift. Others have descended into understandable cynicism. And some know that, while their accustomed practices may seem to the outsider like an antique show, full of '57 Camaros and '72 Mustangs (please correct for desirable cars!), they know that the old models still purr and at least get the road results they want.

A part of the problem can be described as the time/transformation ratio, or how much time teachers are being granted to make a major intellectual and psychological change. If I didn't have the accounts from teachers whose veracity I trust, I would be hard-pressed to believe their tales of demands made upon them for instant changes—changes decreed for the next year, the next semester, or even the next marking period.

Some have especially come to dread their leaders' annual conventions, since there chairs, principals, and superintendents are instantaneously converted to whatever is CCC—Current Curricular Chic—from teachable moments to sung phonics. They fear checking their mailboxes or even their desk corners lest they find there the following Monday a convention handout with the penciled comment across the top: "Starting tomorrow, this is our course of study."

They cannot believe the psychological and intellectual naïveté of their leaders who seem to have no knowledge whatsoever of what is required to effect the transformation of a classroom, a school, or a district—not to mention a teacher's mind. For a major change in any of these, many of us believe that the minimum length required is five to seven years of the most tender and concerted efforts by all involved, from teacher and administrator to child, parent, school board member, and general public. In a 1995 issue of *Primary Voices*, a new NCTE publication, Christine Kline and all involved members of the Hanover Township School District, New Jersey, describe how such a transformation occurred and the seven years it required. And recently, those responsible for the national math standards have stated that they now believe a generation, twenty-five years, will be required to transform the mathematics curriculum in American schools.

This naïveté is especially worrisome since it is so often accompanied by an authoritarian, top-down pattern of proposed change. Some teachers claim that the leaders who demand those changes often seem unaware of the theoretical implications of their recommendations, such as their possible shaky or atheoretical nature; or of the dubious sequence represented by any practice preceding any explicit consideration of theory. Many administrators, the teachers claim, are even seemingly innocent of any theoretical knowledge at all.

For so many teachers now who are theory literate, the situation, of course, is particularly ironic. They know, even though they may not be consulted, the validity or invalidity of the proposed change.

The case of the interactive classroom and curriculum, particularly as set forth so cleanly and clearly in this text by Jeff Golub, marks a happy exception to all these negativities. For the sophisticated and experienced teacher, what is being proposed here already matches her best ongoing practice. She has long served as a designer and director of curricular activities. She already encourages collaborative learning, especially through classroom talk. She steadily sponsors her students' active learning through their composing, comprehending, negotiating, and communicating of meaning.

As to the underlying theory for the interactive classroom, she is reassured about its validity. If she is of a certain age, she probably remembers first reading about meaning-making in chapter six of Postman and Weingartner's influential 1969 text, *Teaching as a Subversive Activity.* And as she continued to reach through the years, she learned of ever stronger support for how she has long taught.

For underlying the interactive classroom and its principles for learning and teaching is the powerful dominant theory in American education today: the national standards in mathematics and science explicitly mention their adherence. Indeed, it qualifies as a dominant theory in the social sciences, such as anthropology and sociology, as well as in the physical sciences. That theory is constructivism, the philosophy and psychology of learning that claims that all of us actively construct our understandings of ourselves, of others, of the world.

Historically, constructivism is either a very old or a relatively new theory, depending, as always, upon the criteria we elect to use as markers. One theorist suggests that we can go back to the philosopher Giambattista Vico in 1710 to find statements that are clearly constructivist in intent.[1] In *Acts of Meaning* (1990), Jerome Bruner gives us a sophisticated history of psychology and provides constructivism with a lineage that includes Pierce, Dewey, and the other original American Pragmatists: such Continental Structuralists as Piaget and such contemporary symbolic constructivists (my term) as Nelson Goodman. To these can justly be added other symbolic constructivists such as Susanne Langer and such neo-Pragmatists as Richard Rorty and Cornel West. Quite a heritage!

In this possibly overelaborate effort to give theoretical reassurance, have I forgotten the heart of Jeff's book, this anthology of activities for an interactive classroom? I hope not, because two large groups of teachers will be grateful for his creative notions and ideas: both the inexperienced teacher, however persuaded of the value of such a classroom, and the experienced teacher need help in enacting the interactive classroom since so few have ever seen it modeled, perhaps particularly in their own educations.

The witty and specific characterization that Jeff's account sets forth may make possible teachers' sponsorship of the kind of classroom in which not only their students but also they themselves can most happily flourish.

Janet Emig
Sanibel Island

Note

1. Vol Glaserfeld, Ernst. 1984. "An Introduction to Radical Constructivism." In *The Invented Reality*, ed. Paul Watzlawick, pp. 27–28. New York: W. W. North.

Preface

An interactive classroom, as I envision it, is very different from a traditional classroom because it operates according to different assumptions, incorporates different principles, and aims for different goals. The primary curricular goal is not to "cover" topics or facts or other material. Teachers do not view students as being passive receptacles for information. And students do not view the teacher as an information giver and sole possessor of knowledge. Instead, in an interactive classroom, knowledge is constructed, not transmitted: the teacher facilitates active learning by serving as a motivating respondent, reacting to students' meaning-making efforts and pushing students to clarify and elaborate.

Instead of moving through a succession of topics and units and objectives, the interactive classroom focuses on a few fundamental goals such as the following:

- to help students make sense of what they read and see and hear;
- to help students write clearly, creatively, honestly, and persuasively;
- to help students learn to construct, comprehend, negotiate, and communicate meanings;
- to make students responsible for their own interpretations.

Instead of "covering" topics and content, the teacher and students work with these goals in mind to "*un*-cover" the curriculum. Every classroom activity is designed to focus on one or more of the preceding goals and to move the students just a little bit closer to the attainment of the overall goal of improved language performance.

The idea of an interactive classroom—with its different approach to instruction—has been developing for me over the past several years. The various parts that go into making up this concept have come from my educational training, my contacts and conversations with colleagues, and my own work with students in the classroom. I learned from my graduate study of speech communication about the importance of students' *own* talk as a vehicle for learning. My participation in the English Coalition Conference in July 1987 focused my attention on the goal of helping students construct meanings in their reading and writing.

As I brought these insights and influences to bear on my classroom teaching, I found myself acting in the classroom as a designer and director instead of an information giver. I designed and conducted activities that engaged students in performance with language while I served as respondent, reacting to students' emerging insights. Many of the activities I have used in this way are described in this book.[1]

In the first chapter the assumptions and principles and goals of an interactive classroom are described and illustrated. Reading this segment will be like looking at the whole picture of a jigsaw puzzle before you set about examining the individual pieces and putting them together. Besides giving you the overall picture of the characteristics of an interactive approach to instruction, the first chapter also identifies the common features and goals of the many activities that will be described in the rest of the book.

Once you have read that far, you can go to any other chapter, in any order, for specific activities of special interest to you. I have deliberately avoided labeling the activities as being appropriate for specific grade levels. I have used many of these activities successfully at both junior and senior high school levels, and I encourage you to try them out and see which ones work best for you and your students. The "Mr. Rogers" exercise, for instance, in which students write to explain a concept to a young child, may seem most appropriate for use at the junior high/middle school level, but I have also used this assignment with my precollege writing classes at Shorecrest High School in Seattle to heighten my students' awareness of their audience as they write.

No matter which activities you choose to conduct in your classroom, you should find that they all adhere to the principles of an interactive classroom as identified in the first chapter. You should also discover that when your students are engaged in these activities, they will talk in class more than you do. This is just one of the characteristics of the interactive classroom that sets it apart from the traditional approach to teaching and learning.

Note

1. Throughout the book, instructions spoken directly to students will always appear enclosed within quotation marks, as in dialogue, to distinguish them from instructions directed to teachers.

Acknowledgments

The idea of an interactive approach to instruction, with its assumptions and principles and goals, evolved for me over a period of several years. As part of my graduate study at the University of Washington, in Seattle, I investigated ways in which students' classroom talk functioned as a vehicle for learning, and I am most appreciative of the encouragement and support provided me at the time by three of my professors, John Stewart, Don Boileau, and Eugene Smith.

Other aspects of the interactive classroom developed through my conversations and connections with my colleagues at NCTE conferences and professional meetings. Two colleagues especially, Louann Reid and Janet Emig, influenced my thinking in this area, and I am grateful to them both. Louann and I worked together on several projects, including a couple of published articles and numerous conference presentations. My own thinking became clarified and "new and improved" because of our many conversations and collaborative presentations, and I am most grateful to Louann for her insightful revisions of my rough-draft thoughts.

One summer, Janet Emig supervised my reading of texts which deal with the concept of "constructivism." She was most supportive, suggesting books to read and taking time to respond to my notes; my insights from this reading and responding convinced me that the process of "constructing meanings" should be the focus of an interactive approach to English instruction. I am appreciative of Janet's continuing encouragement and friendship.

I wish to express my appreciation to all of my students over the years who put up with their teacher's constantly bringing in all sorts of activities and projects, usually signaled by the statement, "Hey! I've got an idea! Let's try this and see if it works!" Almost all of the activities included in this volume were tried out and made "new and improved" in my classroom in response to my students' performance and feedback.

Some of the activities I designed myself. Others I have found or adapted from diverse sources. I have tried to acknowledge the particular sources of the various activities within the chapters themselves, but if I have neglected somewhere to give proper credit where it is due, I hope that readers will bring this oversight to my attention so that corrections can be made.

I received considerable help with the manuscript itself. Melissa Beall, Virginia O'Keefe, and Linda Shadiow, three good friends and colleagues, read and responded to an early draft of the first four chapters. I thank them for their time and effort; their feedback was most helpful. Malia Kapono, Steven Loach, and Jann Rowe, three outstanding English teachers in the Tampa Bay area, volunteered to read and respond to the whole manuscript while they were enrolled in one of my graduate classes at the University of South Florida; their comments were pertinent and insightful, and I am most appreciative of their encouraging words. And I wish to thank Sue Allen and Terry Bigelow for their help in responding to the introduction and to specific chapters of the manuscript.

This is also an appropriate place to thank my parents for their support, especially at crucial times during my career. I am grateful to them for their continuing belief in the worth of what I am doing both in the classroom and in the profession.

And finally, my thanks and deep appreciation to Roy Alin, who served as my supervising teacher during my student-teaching internship. It was Roy who first taught me that "Good teaching is knowing the options," and he has been watching over me and helping me expand my range of instructional choices ever since. This book shows what I have learned.

1 Principles of an Interactive Classroom

An "interactive classroom" is more than a catchy phrase or the latest fad. It is a way of teaching and learning, a reflection of a philosophy of education that provides certain answers to the following questions: (1) What's worth knowing and doing? (2) How do students learn? (3) What is the role or function of the teacher? It might help to explain the characteristics of an interactive classroom by showing what it looks and sounds like, so let's begin by looking at two teachers in two classrooms who are both using an interactive approach to instruction.

Gary, a teacher of sophomore English classes, wants his students to develop some insight into the main characters of Shakespeare's *Romeo and Juliet*, the play they're reading this semester. In addition, he wants to engage his students in writing an effective persuasive essay. So, one day, after his students have nearly finished reading the play, he begins the class by having each student answer this question in writing: "To what extent are Romeo and Juliet truly 'star-crossed' lovers? To what extent was their fate the result of their own actions and poor judgment, and to what extent were they victims of circumstances beyond their control?" Students are asked to take a position on this issue and defend it with specific examples and detailed explanation.

Gary allows the students time in class to draft their response to this question. While they're writing, Gary is not taking attendance or grading papers or creating a new bulletin-board display in the back of the room. Instead, he is busy writing his *own* response to the question so that he, too, will have something to share with the class in the next part of this exercise. After 30 minutes have passed, Gary directs the students to begin the next step of this activity:

> "Pass your paper to the person on your right, and read what that person has written. Then add your response to the paper. Perhaps you disagree with what the writer has said; maybe you

Portions of this chapter appeared in Golub, Jeffrey N. 1992. "New Assumptions, New Assessment in an Interactive Classroom." *Florida English Journal* 28.1 (Spring): 5–7. Used by permission of *Florida English Journal*.

are confused about a point that was made. Whatever your response, engage that writer in a conversation through your comments. When you are finished, pass that paper along to the next person on your right. In this way, the papers will move around the room, each person adding his or her own comments and insights to the growing dialogue and exchange of views. If a paper is passed to you for your comments, but you are still writing on another student's essay, simply pass that second paper long to the next person without comment. Someone, somewhere, will have just finished commenting on one paper and will be ready to read and respond to this next one."

The passing of papers in this way continues for the rest of the period. With only 5 minutes left, students are directed to return the papers to the original writer, the person who wrote the initial draft. Through this activity, students gain insight into the validity and persuasiveness of their position on the topic by reading the exchange of dialogue that followed their initial writing. Students find out through the ensuing responses where they were unclear or unconvincing. They learn about issues they hadn't considered in their discussion and can take these and other insights into account when they revise their papers, thus strengthening the persuasiveness of their arguments.

This classroom activity incorporates some important principles and assumptions of an interactive approach to instruction, an approach designed to help students improve their performance with language:

1. The activity engages students in authentic communication in which they write for a real audience and a real purpose. Students are writing to persuade their classmates, and the ensuing exchange of dialogue is real and honest because students are well aware that they are writing *to* each other, confirming, disagreeing, elaborating, and arguing. They come to understand through this activity that writing is indeed an act of communication closely related to talking. Through the exchange of dialogue, students are indeed "talking" to each other, and it is a genuine and helpful conversation, one that offers the student writers significant insight into the topic under discussion.

The importance of a context and community for students' language performance was one of the conclusions of the English Coalition Conference held in July 1987:

> Learning to speak, think, write, read and interpret texts is not a static process, such as memorizing the five types of paragraphs. Such thinking trivializes the central importance of

> language as communication which must take place in the con-
> text of a community. That is, language learning is a social act, an
> act of connecting or communicating with others outside of the
> self. To ignore the context of language learning is to deny
> growth of the individual and the individual in society. ("English
> for the '90s," 5)

A distinguishing characteristic of an interactive classroom and approach to learning is its provision for a "context of language learning."
Situations and problems and activities, as in the example above, are
designed which enable students to communicate to real audiences for
real purposes. The classroom becomes a "community" of language
users as students interact with each other and with the teacher, constructing, connecting, collaborating, communicating.

2. Gary's exercise involves students in constructing meanings
through language, one of the primary purposes and activities of an
English class. In their initial draft, students express a tentative interpretation of the essay question; then, by responding to the ideas of
others and later, by reading the responses of classmates to their own
initial thoughts, students come to modify and revise and elaborate on
their own meaning. The exercise engages students in *negotiating and
communicating meanings,* and does so by having students take an active
role in their own learning. Students learn to be persuasive, not by
memorizing or following rigid rules or formulas for a persuasion
paper, but by actively engaging in the creation of persuasive arguments and dialogue. It is the difference between learning to play soccer
by either memorizing all the rules of the game (and then having to
pass a multiple-choice test on those rules) and simply getting out there
on the field and kicking the ball around and practicing the critical
skills involved in the game. This exercise encourages students to *perform* with language and then gauge the success of their performance
by studying the feedback their performance generated.

3. Gary's function as teacher has changed in this exercise. He is
not operating here in the traditional teacher role of a giver of information. Instead, he becomes a learner, too, writing his own initial
thoughts on the essay question and seeking feedback right along with
his students. In this way, Gary has created a *community* of learners and
writers and communicators, and he functions in the classroom simply
as one of those learners. His views can be challenged and confirmed
and refuted, and he can learn from these kinds of responses.

4. Another way in which Gary's function has changed is that he is working as a *designer* and *director* instead of as the main actor in the classroom. Think for a moment of a real director of a real play. Who does the actual acting on stage? It's not the director. The director supplies the vision and insight that brings about a worthwhile finished product, but he or she accomplishes this task by moving the actors around, suggesting and coaching and commenting throughout. And Gary's instructional activity proceeds in the same way: Gary directs the students as they move through the stages of the exercise, but it is the students themselves who do the negotiating of meanings, the talking and writing . . . and learning.

Now let's look in on a second classroom as Judy, a middle school teacher, introduces her students to a new poem as part of a poetry unit she is conducting. Judy hands out copies of the poem to the students and then reads it aloud. She then immediately asks each student to write down three questions they have about this poem: "The questions can be about a certain word or a whole line or even about the entire poem, but they should be three questions that you are really concerned about." Once the students have written their questions, they are directed to assemble in small groups, share their questions with their classmates, and try to get satisfactory answers through discussion. After about 30 minutes of this activity, the teacher brings the students together again as a whole class and asks if there are any questions remaining that the students still have about the poem. These questions are dealt with in a whole-class discussion.

As a final activity in the poetry unit, Judy will hand out a new poem and ask students, working in pairs, to write a response to the poem that includes answers to two questions: (1) "What is the meaning of the poem for you?" (2) "How do you know?" Each pair of students will have time in class to confer and will hand in one paper with both names on it.

In the preceding exercises, Judy incorporates another principle of an interactive classroom: she uses the students' own classroom talk as a vehicle for learning. Like Gary, the teacher in the first example, Judy acts as designer and director, setting up an activity in which the students participate in their own learning. It is the students who do the work at hand, constructing meanings for the poem by interacting with their classmates. The teacher can help by questioning and probing the students' responses, thus making the students responsible for their own meanings, but she does not serve as "information giver."

The importance of students' classroom talk for learning purposes has been recognized for some time now. James Britton (1975) wrote about it almost twenty years ago:

> The relationship of talk to writing is central to the writing process ... good talk helps to encourage good writing. It is probable that of all the things teachers are now doing to make their pupils' approach to writing more stimulating, and the writing itself seem a more integral part of the manifold activities of the classroom, it is the encouragement of different kinds of talk which is the commonest and most productive factor. (29)

In completing the written assignments, students use their talking as a way of, in Britton's words, "assimilating the task to their own understanding":

> Talk is more expressive ... talk relies on an immediate link with listeners, usually a group or a whole class; the rapid exchanges of conversation allow many things to go on at once—exploration, clarification, shared interpretation, insight into differences of opinion, illustration and anecdote, explanation by gesture, expression of doubt; and if something is not clear you can go on until it is. (29)

"Doing English" is a process of constructing, comprehending, negotiating, and communicating meanings, and students' classroom talk is one way in which this process is accomplished. An interactive approach encourages students to move freely between "thought" and "meaning" and "word" as they talk to each other about the task at hand. Margaret Donaldson (1979) reinforces Britton's point that students' talk does not simply allow for the "discovery" of meanings; rather, it actually permits the *construction* of meanings:

> [T]here is a whole set of very fundamental notions about the ways in which we relate to the world. Of these, the most important is the idea that this relation is *active* on our part from the beginning. We do not just sit and wait for the world to impinge on us. We try actively to interpret it, to make sense of it. We grapple with it, we construe it intellectually, *we represent it to ourselves.* (67)

"Making sense" of the world through language is an important goal of an English class; and students' talk is one of the main tools involved in this process. A corollary of this principle, then, is the encouragement of *collaborative learning* in the interactive classroom. Two students working together on the writing of a single paper are not cheating— they're *learning*. The talk that passes between them in the preparation and drafting of the paper allows for the brainstorming and rehearsal of lots of ideas.

Summary

An interactive classroom:

- provides an appropriate and worthwhile context for students' language performance, allowing students to communicate in both oral and written modes for real audiences and real purposes;
- uses students' classroom talk as a vehicle for learning;
- encourages collaborative learning;
- focuses on the creating, comprehending, negotiating, and communicating of meanings;
- casts the teacher in the role of designer and director of instructional activities.

Some years ago I heard a remark that now seems to be especially pertinent and insightful: "Don't evaluate teachers based on what they do in the classroom; instead, judge them on the basis of what they allow their *students* to do." This, then, is a book of classroom activities for *students* to do, activities that engage students in authentic, appropriate, and worthwhile communication situations. The activities in the following chapters are certainly varied and wide-ranging, but they all share two features:

1. They display and exemplify one or more principles of the interactive approach; and
2. They focus on what the *students* are doing and learning.

These are classroom activities that allow students to construct meanings and connect and collaborate and communicate with each other. This is how one's language and communication competence develops in the world outside the classroom; and so we recreate that outside world inside the classroom, establishing a classroom community of learners and language users. This is what the interactive classroom is all about.

Works Cited

Britton, James, et al. 1975. *The Development of Writing Abilities (11–18)*. London: Macmillan.

Donaldson, Margaret. 1979. *Children's Minds.* New York: W. W. Norton.

"English for the '90s and Beyond." 1987. Final report prepared by the Secondary Strand. English Coalition Conference. Queenstown, Maryland.

Golub, Jeffrey N. 1992. "New Assumptions, New Assessment in an Interactive Classroom." *Florida English Journal* 28.1 (Spring): 5–7.

2 Establishing a Positive Classroom Climate

It is important that the students feel comfortable with each other in the classroom. Since they will be interacting frequently with their classmates, they should be provided opportunities early on to get to know a little something about each other. The following activities can help. They offer opportunities for classroom interaction, the building of a positive classroom climate, and the introduction of concepts and skills that will be used throughout the course.

"Warm Fuzzies"

An important element in any classroom climate is the manner in which students see and treat each other. Student interaction at all times should reflect an attitude of courtesy and respect, especially in a course focusing on something as personal as one's developing language and communication behavior. Introducing the concept of "warm fuzzies" will help establish a positive attitude and climate at the beginning of the course, a climate that will last throughout the year.

In 1977, Claude Steiner published a wonderful story about "warm fuzzies" and "cold pricklies." Each year when I was teaching at the junior high school level, I read this story aloud to my students on the first day of class in September.

Here's the story:

The Original "Warm Fuzzy Tale"*

Once upon a time, a long time ago, there lived two very happy people called Tim and Maggi with their two children, John and Lucy. To understand how happy they were, you have to understand how things were in those days.

---

*Reprinted from *The Original Warm Fuzzy Tale,* by Claude Steiner. Copyright © 1977 by B. L. Winch & Associates/Jalmar Press. Used with permission from B. L. Winch & Associates/Jalmar Press.

You see, in those happy days everyone was given at birth a small, soft Fuzzy Bag. Anytime a person reached into this bag he was able to pull out a Warm Fuzzy.

Warm Fuzzies were very much in demand because whenever somebody was given a Warm Fuzzy it made him feel warm and fuzzy all over.

People who didn't get Warm Fuzzies regularly were in danger of developing a sickness in their backs which caused them to shrivel up and die.

In those days it was very easy to get Warm Fuzzies. Anytime that somebody felt like it, he might walk up to you and say, "I'd like to have a Warm Fuzzy."

You would then reach into your bag and pull out a Fuzzy the size of a little girl's hand. As soon as the Fuzzy saw the light of day it would smile and blossom into a large, shaggy Warm Fuzzy.

You then would lay it on the person's shoulder or head or lap and it would snuggle up and melt right against their skin and make them feel good all over.

People were always asking each other for Warm Fuzzies, and since they were always given freely, getting enough of them was never a problem.

There were always plenty to go around, and as a consequence everyone was happy and felt warm and fuzzy most of the time.

One day a bad witch became angry because everyone was so happy and no one was buying potions and salves.

The witch was very clever and devised a very wicked plan.

One beautiful morning the witch crept up to Tim while Maggi was playing with their daughter and whispered in his ear, "See here, Tim, look at all the Fuzzies that Maggi is giving to Lucy. You know, if she keeps it up, eventually she is going to run out and then there won't be any left for you."

Tim was astonished. He turned to the witch and said, "Do you mean to tell me that there isn't a Warm Fuzzy in our bag every time we reach into it?"

And the witch said, "No, absolutely not, and once you run out, that's it. You don't have any more." With this, the witch flew away, laughing and cackling.

Tim took this to heart and began to notice every time Maggi gave up a Warm Fuzzy to somebody else. Eventually he got very worried and upset because he liked Maggi's Warm Fuzzies very much and did not want to give them up. He certainly did not think it was right for Maggi to be spending all her Warm Fuzzies on the children and on other people.

He began to complain every time he saw Maggi giving a Warm Fuzzy to somebody else, and because Maggi liked him very much, she stopped giving Warm Fuzzies to other people as often and reserved them for him.

The children watched this and soon began to get the idea that it was wrong to give up Warm Fuzzies any time you were asked or felt like it.

They too became very careful. They would watch their parents closely, and whenever they felt that one of their parents was giving too many Fuzzies to others, they also began to object. They began to feel worried whenever they gave away too many Warm Fuzzies.

Even though they found a Warm Fuzzy every time they reached into their bag, they reached in less and less and became more and more stingy. Soon people began to notice the lack of Warm Fuzzies, and they began to feel less warm and less fuzzy. They began to shrivel up, and, occasionally, people would die from lack of Warm Fuzzies.

More and more people went to the witch to buy potions and salves even though they didn't seem to work.

Well, the situation was getting very serious indeed. The bad witch didn't really want the people to die (since dead people couldn't buy salves and potions) so a new plan was devised.

Everyone was given a bag that was very similar to the Fuzzy Bag except that this one was cold while the Fuzzy Bag was warm. Inside of the witch's bag were Cold Pricklies. These Cold Pricklies did not make people feel warm and fuzzy, but made them feel cold and prickly instead.

But they did prevent peoples' backs from shriveling up. So, from then on, everytime somebody said, "I want a Warm Fuzzy," people who were worried about depleting their supply would say, "I can't give you a Warm Fuzzy, but would you like a Cold Prickly?"

Sometimes, two people would walk up to each other, thinking they could get a Warm Fuzzy, but one or the other of them would change his mind and they would wind up giving each other Cold Pricklies. So while very few people were dying, a lot of people were still unhappy and feeling very cold and Prickly.

The situation got very complicated. Warm Fuzzies, which used to be thought of as free as air, became extremely valuable. This caused people to do all sorts of things in order to obtain them.

Before the witch had appeared, people used to gather in groups of three or four or five, never caring too much who was giving Warm Fuzzies to whom. After the coming of the witch, people began to pair off and to reserve all their Warm Fuzzies for each other exclusively. People who forgot themselves and gave a Fuzzy to someone else would feel guilty because they knew that their partner would probably resent the loss. People who could not find a generous partner had to buy their Fuzzies and they worked long hours to earn the money.

Another thing which happened was that some people would take Cold Pricklies—which were limitless and freely available—coat them white and fluffy, and pass them on as Warm Fuzzies.

These counterfeit Warm Fuzzies were really Plastic Fuzzies, and they caused additional difficulties. For instance, two people would get together and freely exchange Plastic Fuzzies, which presumably should have made them feel good, but they came away feeling bad instead. Since they thought they had been exchanging Warm Fuzzies, people grew very confused about this, never realizing that their cold, prickly feelings were really the result of the fact that they had been given a lot of Plastic Fuzzies.

So the situation was very, very dismal, and it all started because of the coming of the witch who made people believe that some day, when least expected, they might reach into their Warm Fuzzy Bag and find no more.

Not long ago, a lovely, strong woman with big hips and a happy smile came to this unhappy land.

She seemed not to have heard about the witch and was not worried about running out of Warm Fuzzies.

She gave them out freely, even when not asked. People called her the Hip Woman and some disapproved of her because she was giving the children the idea that they should not worry about running out of Warm Fuzzies.

The children liked her very much because they felt good around her. They, too, began to give out Warm Fuzzies whenever they felt like it.

The grownups became concerned and decided to pass a law to protect the children from using up their supplies of Warm Fuzzies. The law made it a criminal offense to give out Warm Fuzzies in a reckless manner, without a license.

Many children, however, seemed not to know or care, and in spite of the law they continued to give each other Warm Fuzzies whenever they felt like it and always when asked.

Because there were many many children—almost as many as grownups—it began to look as if maybe the children would have their way.

As of now it is hard to say what will happen. Will the forces of law and order stop the children? Are the grownups going to join with the Hip Woman and the children in taking a chance that there will always be as many Warm Fuzzies as needed?

Will Tim and Maggi, recalling the days when they were so happy and when Warm Fuzzies were unlimited, begin to give away Warm Fuzzies freely again?

The struggle spread all over the land and is probably going on right where you live. If you want to, and I hope you do, you can join by freely giving and asking for Warm Fuzzies and by being as loving and healthy as you can.

The End

Warm fuzzies are statements you make or things you do that make another person feel worthwhile, appreciated, and . . . well, . . . warm and fuzzy. They must be given sincerely, of course, but they should be given frequently and certainly whenever appropriate. Students come to understand this point readily and will soon begin to model your behavior if you give warm fuzzies yourself. It is interesting to hear students respond to a classmate's occasional "cutting" remark by saying, "That's a 'cold prickly.'" Making students aware of warm fuzzies is a way to help them fulfill a basic human need to feel good about oneself. Students need to know that they have the power to "warm fuzzy" each other and that it is perfectly acceptable to do so.

With some classes I have gone one step further to reinforce the concept of "warm fuzzies." I followed up an oral reading and discussion of the story by directing students to *bring in* a warm fuzzy the next week. Invariably there is one student who asks, "But what does one *look* like?" and I respond, "I don't know. I won't know that until I see what you bring in." And the warm fuzzies that those students created were fantastic! Large, stuffed balls of hair or fur with plastic eyes; glass jars enclosed in soft sponge material. One student even brought in a giant lampshade topped with a tuft of wavy hair. Having students work to construct a visual, concrete representation of a warm fuzzy is a fun way to lead them to focus on the concept and see it as an acceptable, worthwhile, positive element in their classroom conduct.

I want to explain the importance of warm fuzzies as a basic human need. This explanation begins with an analogy and relies on a *transactional* view of how our self-image develops. Think first of how we see ourselves physically. Do you realize that it is impossible for us to see our own face? We have to look outward—in this case, at a mirror—and gaze at our *reflection* in order for us to see ourselves. In the same way, our self-image—our "picture" of ourselves—develops in response to *how we see others seeing us*. It is *other people* who contribute to our feelings of self-worth through their "reflections" of us, their responses to our behavior and communication efforts. Given this perspective, one can see the importance of warm fuzzies. Each student in class serves as a mirror for everyone else, and a positive classroom climate depends upon positive reflections (in the form of "warm fuzzies") being given frequently and honestly by these "mirrors." Students are more likely to contribute to, and maintain, a positive classroom climate this way if they are made aware of the importance of this basic human need *and* that they have the power to fulfill it for each other.

What Does English Deal With?

Ellen Turlington Johnston-Hale, a poet-in-residence in North Carolina and a consultant in twenty-two other states, wrote a wonderful poem (see Johnston 1976) that considers the question, "What does English deal with?"

We Don't Do *Nothin'* in Here![**]

> Today
> a small sparrow
perched on a slanted window pane,
peeking, upside down, into my classroom.
Before I'd even seen the little eavesdropper,
>> three students shouted,
>>> "HEY!

[**]From *We Don't Do Nothin' in Here,* by Ellen Turlington Johnston. Copyright © 1976 by Moore Publishing Company. Used by permission of the author.

There's a POEM, Miz. J!"
Sure enough, it *was* —
a real class-stopper.
They wrote in their "Polaroids,"
(the little note-pads
they take "word-pictures" in),
of freedom,
and boredom,
and upside-down,
and flight.
The poems sprouted
left and right.
About then, this voice piped up, loud and clear:
"I signed up for *English*.
When're we gonna do some ENGLISH in here?!?"

Today
we skipped backwards
to when we were very young,
and see-sawed,
and blind-man-bluffed at twilight,
and sang out OLLEY-OLLEY-OXEN-ALL-IN-FREE.
And I told them how
the principle happiness for me,
when I was six,
was my l'il Orphan Annie decoder pin.
Then, they remembered again
the wonder of home-made mud pies,
and magic wands that used to be sticks.
We wrote of tadpole pets
that — O! happy surprise —
turned to frogs . . . overnight;
and of floppity red-headed Raggedy Anns,
and three-wheelers,
and first patent-leathers shoes,
spittin' bright.
Children again, we spun our wonderment
into shimmering nets of words, there.
Again, the voice: "This is 'sposed to be *English*.
So when're we gonna ever do some ENGLISH in here?!?"

Today
we hobbled ahead
to very, very old.
We wrote of grandmothers,
great-uncles,
arthritis,
of tales told, told, and *re*told;
and of the musty smell of old,

and the thin-ness.
"His baggy trousers lapped around his ankles,"
         Mary wrote.
  When she read it to us, I got goose-bumply cold.
     (So did quite a few others.)
       We wrote about lonely . . .
  "The eyes, outlets of many visions,
    how tired and forgotten."
We wove words into tapestries of bony fingers,
   trembling hands with brown spots,
     and lavendar shawls.

      Today
   we played with words.
We found sixty-eight — count 'em — in all —
    to use for "said,"
  to show how someone *feels;*
like: they shout or exclaim or whimper or groan . . .
   Words flew like confetti in there.
Then . . . the voice again . . . demanding:
  "But when're we gonna have some *English*?"

    "English?"

    "Yeah. Nouns 'n adjectives.
     Diagraming.
      ENGLISH!
We don't do NOTHIN' in here!"

Each student who enters your class in the fall has a different answer to this question of what English deals with.[1, 2] Some of the students may even see English in the same way as the pupil complaining in the poem. Their answers may well be different from *your* answer, too, which means that their expectations about the course content and instructional approach will differ, also. So it's important to consider this question with the students right at the beginning of the course. In this way, students will be encouraged to reflect on what it is they will be studying and learning and doing . . . and *why.*

Step 1. Have students get into small groups of 4 people each. Hand out to each person a large sheet of construction paper and a felt pen. Instruct *each* student to *draw* a picture that shows or represents what, in his or her opinion, English deals with.

Step 2. After students have drawn their pictures, they should share them with the other members of their group by following this procedure: Each student in turn holds up his or her picture for the others to see. The other members first make statements about what the artist was trying to show or communicate, and then the picture's owner responds to their "guesses" by commenting on the accuracy of their remarks and provides further explanation of the points he or she was trying to make in the drawing. After all members of the group have shared their drawings in this way, the pictures should be mounted on the classroom walls.

Step 3. Hand out small index cards (3 x 5) to each student and direct the class to write a short statement about what English deals with. The statement may consist of more than one sentence, but it must all fit on the front side of the card. Students should work individually in completing their statements. Collect the cards, and read some of the statements aloud (without mentioning the authors' names). You might post some of the cards on the classroom walls, also.

Step 4. There are a couple of possibilities here for procedures to follow in making the point of this exercise clear to students. One way is to share with students *your* perception of what English deals with and compare your perspective with theirs. This exercise has raised their consciousness about the content of English class, and they have engaged in a kind of "negotiation of meanings" with their classmates. They are ready, then, to "negotiate" with you in an attempt to come to a clear understanding of what they will be doing in class and why they will be doing it. Such an understanding will contribute to a feeling of "community" and commitment.

But another way to make the point of this exercise clear to students is *not* to share with students your perspective of what English deals with—at least, not right away. Instead, ask students—periodically throughout the semester and immediately after they have completed certain exercises—what these activities have to do with "English." In this way, you will be leading them to continually revise and reconsider their conception of the "appropriate content and focus for an English class" in the light of new information and experiences. The processes of *assimilation* and *accommodation* will affect each student's perspective, causing it to change and mature. In the last week of class at the end of the semester, return to the exercise described above and run it again. This second time, have students give a more complete response to the question "What does English deal with?" and support their answers by referring to the work they did during the course. Compare students' responses given at the end of the course with those they wrote at the beginning. What has changed?

"Tell us about . . ."

This is a "listening" exercise, one that develops three listening skills simultaneously. Because so many interactive classroom activities involve students in listening to each other (during whole-class discussions, small writing groups, collaborative projects), it is important to introduce and develop these skills early on.

Announce to the class that for the next couple of days, they are going to work on their listening skills. They will need these skills throughout the year, and this activity will make them aware of what good listening really entails.

Have students select a partner for this activity. Distribute to each student a copy of the "Tell us about . . ." sheet that lists possible topics for this exercise (see figure 1).[3] Explain that one person in each pair will select a topic from this sheet and begin talking about it to his or her partner. While the person is talking, the partner will practice these three listening skills: (1) *focusing,* (2) *drawing out* the person through questions, and (3) *listening without judging.*[4, 5] Describe to the students how these skills are applied in the activity:

> *Focusing:* "While Odalys is talking about her subject, Steve will keep the focus of attention on *her.* The focus is lost if, for instance, Odalys says at one point: 'I took a trip to New York last summer,' and Steve immediately replies, 'Oh, I went there once, too! Let me tell you about it!' Keep the focus on the person who is speaking."

> *Drawing out the person through questions:* "As Odalys talks, Steve will occasionally ask her questions that he may have about some aspect of her subject. These questions will show Odalys that Steve has indeed been listening to her—How can you ask an appropriate question about something if you haven't really been listening to the speaker?—and that he is interested in what she is saying and wants to know more. So Steve is going to have to listen carefully as Odalys talks. Perhaps he will hear something that is not clear to him, or he might find that he wants additional details about something particularly interesting. In either case, Steve will ask questions and let Odalys know in this way that he is following her talk and is sincerely interested in what she has to say."

> *Listening without judging:* "This is the most difficult skill to master. Imagine Odalys telling about a time when she skipped class

Tell Us about

How you spend your free time on weekends.

Something that you can do now that you couldn't do a year ago.

How you helped someone once.

What you look for in choosing a friend.

Something that you are proud of that you have written, drawn, or made.

Something good that has happened as a result of a choice you made.

Something important that you are planning to do.

Whether you prefer to make choices yourself or have others make choices for you.

Something you are proud of that you have worked hard for.

Something good you have done that not many people know about.

A difficult choice you made recently.

Something you did that took courage to do.

Something important you decided in which you made the choice all by yourself.

Something difficult that you learned which you are proud of.

Who you go to for advice when making important or difficult decisions.

Something that you have done before that you would do differently today.

A choice you made that did not work out the way you had hoped.

A change you would like to make in yourself.

Something about a choice you made that turned out well.

A choice you had to make between two things you wanted very much.

Figure 1. List of suggested topics for the "Tell Us about . . ." activity. Adapted from Howe and Howe (1975, 209–10).

to go downtown with some friends, and Steve replies, 'Well, *that* was a dumb thing to do!' Steve is expressing a *judgment* of Odalys and her actions, and the first time he does this is the *last* time that Odalys will tell him *anything*. Listen without judging, without expressing either approval or disapproval. Simply listen to learn, and ask questions to draw out the person and invite him or her to say more. But don't evaluate what you hear."

After explaining these three skills, direct the pairs of students to begin the exercise: one student in each pair talks about a topic on the sheet while his or her partner listens, practicing the three listening skills. After 15 to 20 minutes have passed, instruct the students to "switch": now the partner selects a topic, and the student who *had* been talking gets a chance to practice the listening skills.

At the end of this activity, ask students for their reactions. Did they feel as if their partner were really listening? How did it feel to have someone really listen this closely, asking appropriate questions and not "judging"?

Repeating this exercise during a few succeeding days and directing students to work with a different partner each time will give them an opportunity to meet and talk with new classmates. Students will have gained an awareness of what is involved in *really* listening. The hard work begins with practicing those skills regularly and frequently throughout the class.

Introduction Speech

Having students introduce one another to the class has always been a good way to get them to see their classmates as real people and to "break the ice" at the beginning of the school year. The traditional procedure for such an exercise, however, could use some improvement: Student "A" interviews student "B" and then "B" turns right around and interviews "A." Nothing much happens, especially since "A" and "B" have been best friends for years and already know each other well. No new meetings or mingling are accomplished this way.

You might try this approach: Have the students find a partner, but one whom they do not know well. Announce that "A" will interview "B", taking the entire class period to do so, if needed. You might spend a few minutes brainstorming some appropriate questions with the class. Get the class to generate topics that they would sincerely like to know about—trips their partner has taken, something important that has occurred in their life—things like that. You might even encourage the interviewer to focus on one or two interesting facets of his or her partner's life instead of employing a "shotgun" approach. In their introduction, interviewers should avoid presenting simply a list such as "Amanda's favorite color is blue; her favorite food is pizza. . . ." This is deadly, dull, and superficial.

On the first day of this exercise, "A" interviews "B", taking notes that will be organized and polished later. This is an information gathering time only. When students come into class the next day, direct those students who were interviewed the previous day to stand on one side of the room and have the "interviewers" move to the other side. New partners are to be chosen today for a second round of interviews: those who *conducted* an interview yesterday must now find someone (from the opposite side of the room) to interview them; and those who *were* interviewed will now conduct their own interview themselves.

They must select new partners, so that no one will be interviewing the same person who interviewed *them*.

On the third day, after all students have conducted an interview and have been interviewed themselves, allow 30 minutes for students to organize their notes and prepare an introduction (and I, as the teacher, participate in this exercise, also). When it is time to begin the introduction speeches, I give my speech first. I have found this approach helpful for a couple of reasons: my introductory speech serves as a model for desired length and quality, and it "breaks the ice"— rarely do students want to be the first one to speak, but they're much more willing to be the second.

The twist to this procedure may be seen in the speaking order: imagine that the teacher stands before the class and introduces Akemi, working from the notes he has compiled and telling what he has learned. Immediately after he finishes his introduction, Akemi stands up and delivers *her* introductory speech. Remember that Akemi interviewed someone other than the person who interviewed *her*. So Akemi introduces Teresa, who then immediately afterward gives *her* speech introducing Carlos, who then . . . and so it goes in an unbroken string of introductions until all have spoken and been introduced. With this approach, the person who has just been introduced becomes visible to the audience immediately afterward as he or she presents the *next* introduction. Once in awhile, the string of introductions is broken: Tenisha introduces James, for instance, but James is absent today, so he obviously cannot present his own speech. In this case, I simply ask for a volunteer to present their introduction at this time, and the chain continues from there; another option in this case is to ask Tenisha to postpone her introduction until James returns to class the next day.

"Something Important" Speech

Here is another opportunity to enable students to learn more about their classmates and get to know each other well. Ask students to bring something to class tomorrow that is *important* to *them*: "Don't bring in Aunt Minnie's $7,000 stamp collection—that's not what I'm talking about. Simply bring in an object—a stuffed animal, a ring, a letter, a picture—something that, for some reason, is very important to you." Sometimes students will bring in a picture of their pet dog or their best friend; others might bring in a baseball glove to *represent* the sport itself that is important.

The next day, when students bring these objects to class, ask for a volunteer to come to the front of the room and say a few words about why the object is important to him or her. Then, the class should be allowed to ask follow-up questions. The next volunteer gives his or her speech, and so it goes until all have had a chance to talk in front of the class. You should find that each speech lasts from 1 to 3 minutes. There's no need for the students to prepare their talk in advance; a strange thing happens when students bring in something that is genuinely important to them: *the words flow.* The students obviously know their subject well and have something to say about it. A reticent speaker will be encouraged to say more and provide details by the follow-up questions from his or her classmates. Students like this exercise because they are encouraged to share something that has become a part of themselves with a friendly, appreciative audience. Often the student's talk ends with a spontaneous, sincere round of applause for the speaker.

This activity provides students a low-risk opportunity to speak in front of a large group, and it often produces some fascinating talks and insights. The speakers care about the exercise because they are sharing something that is really important to them, and the audience is sincerely interested in learning about why the object is of value.

Brainstorming in Small Groups

The practice of brainstorming as a way to generate ideas has been used for years in English classes. It's an activity that demonstrates to students that sometimes good ideas come from interacting with others. This is an important point to emphasize in the beginning of an English class, especially when a collaborative learning and instructional approach will be utilized throughout the year. But brainstorming has other benefits as well: it can be used to build a positive classroom climate; it promotes interaction among classmates; and it can serve as the first step in teaching students to work productively and harmoniously in small groups. The rules for brainstorming are as follows:

> 1. *"The more ideas, the better."* In brainstorming, the goal is to generate as many ideas as possible. Have the brainstorming groups of students create a long list of suggestions and possibilities; the longer the list, the better. The *quality* of the ideas can be evaluated later. At a later time—and in a separate operation—the "bad" ideas can be separated from the "good" ones. But in the beginning, students should consider anything and every-

thing related to the topic being brainstormed. To encourage the production of as many ideas as possible, you might set up a competitive arrangement between the brainstorming groups. After each brainstorming session, ask the recorder in each group to add up all the ideas on his or her list. Write the totals for each group, as reported by the group's recorder, on the board.

2. *"The wilder the ideas, the better."* This is an opportunity for students to think of crazy, silly, outrageous ideas. Such thinking is encouraged in this activity and in this environment. Because students are building on each other's ideas here, one student's "crazy" suggestion may give a classmate a terrific idea that would not have been thought of without the "crazy" stimulus.

3. *"'Hitchhiking' is encouraged."* Brainstorming involves an intense cooperative effort in that students work with each other's ideas and suggestions. Students are encouraged to "hitchhike" on each other's ideas, modifying classmates' suggestions in different ways in order to generate other ideas. With this arrangement, students must be cautioned not to see an idea as "theirs." That great idea they thought of probably arose because of something they heard from a classmate. So whose idea is it, really? All generated ideas should be seen as belonging to the *group,* and all are available for modification and improvement without a need to claim "ownership."

As an example of how "hitchhiking" can work to produce something valuable, I once had a class brainstorm ways to improve a standard piece of classroom furniture, the common student desk. At one point in the brainstorming, I overheard a student in one group say, "Throw it off the face of the earth." Immediately another student exclaimed, "Hey! Let's put a map of the earth *in* the desk, right on the top desk part." And another student added to this idea, "Yeah, and we can have rollers that you can use to turn the map to any part of the earth you want to see." This is a nice idea, and it came about because of the original suggestion to throw the desk off the face of the earth. You can use this example with students to show them how *wild* ideas and *hitchhiking* can work together to produce something that later proves to be pertinent, practical, and valuable.

4. *"No evaluation of ideas during brainstorming."* This is the rule that makes everything else possible. If students were to evaluate ideas as they were being generated, the process would quickly

come to a halt. Imagine a student offering a suggestion, only to be told, *"That's* not on the topic," or "That's stupid!" That would be the last time the student would offer *anything.* Who wants to risk being told that their idea is "wrong" or "silly"? Simply instruct the group recorders to write down *everything;* they can evaluate and eliminate *later.*

Procedure for Brainstorming: Each brainstorming session should last 3 minutes—enough time for students to generate lots of ideas, but short enough that students don't get tired or bored with the activity. Each subsequent brainstorming session should have the groups producing a greater number of ideas than they did in the previous one. As the groups are brainstorming, call out the time remaining in 30-second intervals. This keeps the brainstorming going at an intense level of activity. At the end of 3 minutes, direct all groups to stop immediately; have the recorders count the number of brainstormed ideas on their list; and write the totals for each group on the board for everyone to see.

Sample Topics for Brainstorming. The following topics can be used to allow students to practice the brainstorming process[6]:

1. "How many ways can you think of to come to school in the morning?" (Pogo stick, donkey, parachute, rocket ship, walk over the telephone wires, etc.)

2. "Assuming you could change your size and shape, how would you come to school in the morning?" (Change into a drop of water and come to school in the drinking fountain; come to school in a friend's lunch sack; etc.)

3. "How many ways can you think of to have fun with an alligator?" (Put dry ice in his mouth and call the fire department; buy him a big red balloon at the fair; play jump rope with him; etc.)

4. "How many different kinds of *lines* can you think of?" (Lines to be memorized for a drama production; lines on a football field; lines that form as people wait to get into a movie; etc.)

5. "List everything you can think of that is both *soft* and *blue.*" (Melted blue crayons; a fish that is dipped in blue paint; a sad teddy bear; etc.)

6. "Make a list of things that come in, or are associated with, the number three." (Three blind mice; three little pigs; three sides of a triangle; triple-decker sandwich; etc.)

During the first few brainstorming sessions, emphasize only the *number* of ideas generated, trying to get the students to increase the number of ideas suggested and the length of their lists in each subsequent round of brainstorming. Within three or four sessions—each lasting 3 minutes and using different topics each time—you should find that students can generate more than 100 ideas. At this point, you can begin to *look* at some of these ideas by giving additional instructions. Use the following topic for this purpose:

> "Your group is an advertising agency. A certain manufacturer of a popular kind of candy has come to you because it has plans to redesign its product. The manufacturer will change the packaging, for instance, but it also wants to change the *name* of the candy. That's why it has come to you for help. In three minutes, brainstorm possible names for *M & M's candies.*"

At the end of this brainstorming session, have the groups' recorders add up the total number of items on their list, and then give these additional instructions to each group:

> "Go through your list and select three of your *best* names for M & M's candies. These should be ideas that you think are so unique and unusual that they just might work as suitable alternatives to the candy's current name. Take a few minutes to decide which three names on your list you like the best, and then we'll hear these selections from each group."

Building Group Cohesiveness

Once students have become familiar with the brainstorming process and have experienced a few trial runs using the rules and topics listed above, they are ready to do more extensive work in small groups. They will still use the skills they have just practiced, but now their minds are more open to the ideas of playing with possibilities and considering a variety of alternatives. Try the following exercise and project as a follow-up to the initial brainstorming sessions. These two activities will build a sense of cohesiveness among the members of the groups and will allow students to further develop the brainstorming skills they have been practicing.

First, direct each group to brainstorm a group name for itself and then design a shield or logo or picture to represent their group. The design must include all of the students' names somewhere in the picture. Have sheets of construction paper available for this activity. Hang the pictures on the wall near where each group is sitting.

A Brainstorming Project: Ask the students to design a new eating implement that has as important a function as the knife, fork, and spoon. Tell them that this invention belongs on every dining-room table. Have students complete the following tasks:

1. "Design the invention and be prepared to explain to the class how it works. Feel free to draw a picture if you wish."

2. "Give your invention a name."

3. "In an oral presentation, convince the rest of the class that your invention is (a) necessary, (b) practical, and (c) desirable."

4. "Design a magazine ad for your invention." [You might have students write a radio ad, too, and then comment on the differences in the demands and problems encountered in dealing with the two media. Consider also the idea of having students create a TV ad for their product and then act out the ad in front of the class.]

Each group in turn presents its design for a new eating implement to the class, describing how the invention works and persuading the class that the implement is necessary, practical, and desirable. By the time this project is completed, the students will have demonstrated mastery of the brainstorming skills and process, will have become part of a cohesive group, and will be able and ready to use this process to help themselves generate ideas for their writing on subsequent assignments.

Hidden Figures

An important point to establish at the beginning of the course is that students should turn to each other for feedback on their writing efforts. Tell them that one way to tell whether what they've written is "good stuff" is to *show it to other people.* Evaluation of writing is an *interpersonal* matter. We can't run a student's paper through a scantron machine to see what is "correct" or "incorrect." Writing is a *subjective* phenomenon: another mind must judge the writing's appropriateness and creativity, and this "judging" is subjective, not objective. It is difficult for students to evaluate their *own* writing because they are too close to it. But to give it to a classmate for evaluation can often result in helpful comments and suggestions for revision. Students need to find out what parts of their writing are unclear or confusing; what parts are particularly entertaining or insightful or descriptive. Their classmates can provide that information, and the following exercise will make this point clearly.

Hand out the sheet labeled "Hidden Figures" (see figure 2). Direct students' attention to the example in which the number "3" has been "hidden" by making it part of a larger picture, in this case a vase. Instruct students to do the same to each of the other numbers and letters on the page: "hide" them by making them part of a picture or figure or diagram. They may turn the page any way they want in order to complete this task.

Allow 20 to 30 minutes for the drawing. Then give the following instructions:

1. "You have just completed five drawings. But how do you know which ones are really good? Which ones are the most clever or different or unusual? One way you can find out is to ask your classmates. *They* can tell you which ones they like the most, and this is important information for you. It tells you which of your drawings seem to communicate the clearest; which ones are most appreciated and enjoyed by others."

2. "You are going to get this kind of feedback now. In just a moment, I am going to ask you to stand up and move around the room, stopping to look closely at *each* drawing. Carry a pen or pencil with you. If you find a drawing that you particularly like, then *put your initials by it*. Perhaps you like what Rachel has done with the 'K', for instance. Her other drawings aren't anything unusual, but she really did a terrific job with that 'K'. Put your initials by that drawing, and simply ignore the others. If you like two or even three of a person's drawings, put your initials by each of them."

3. "Your initials are something very personal to you. You don't sprinkle them over these drawings like sugar over cereal. Save them for those drawings that you *really* like. When you are all finished, go back to your seat and look again at your own drawings. You will know which of your drawings went over well with the class by the number of initials beside them."

4. "Start now."

You should participate in this exercise along with the students, moving around the room and putting your initials next to those pictures you especially like. After all, your opinion counts, too, and you are part of the audience for students' communication efforts. At the end of the activity, after the students are seated again and have had a chance to see which of their drawings seemed to attract the most initials, you should make the final point: that this is how students can

Hidden Figures

See if you can build a picture around each of the numbers and letters below so that the figure becomes hidden in your drawing. Try to make the figure blend into your drawing so that it cannot be recognized in its original form. The first drawing is done for you.

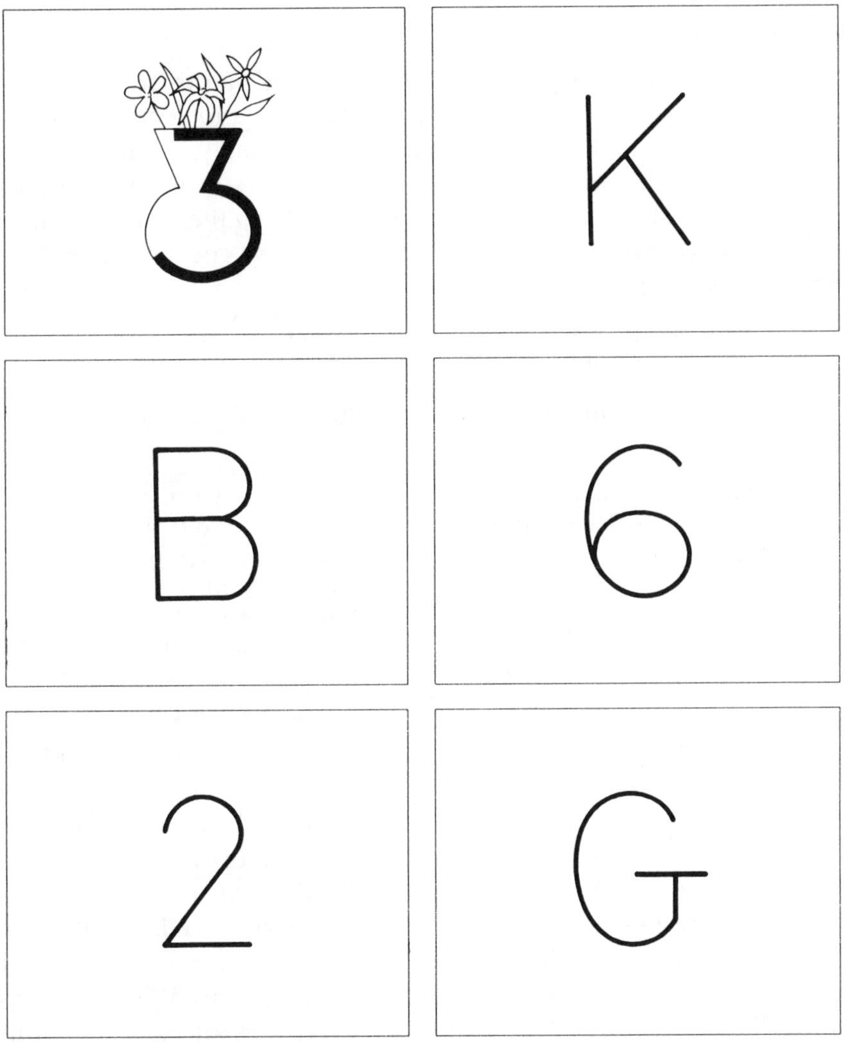

Figure 2. The "Hidden Figures" activity. (Adapted from Renzulli 1973. Copyright © 1973 by Harper & Row Publishers, Inc. Used by permission of HarperCollins Publishers, Inc.)

determine throughout the course the worth of their writing—*show it to their classmates,* gauge their response, and obtain feedback for revision. This exercise serves as a starting point for this practice by letting students see that their classmates' reactions are indeed important as an indication of the success of their communication efforts.

Writing Notes

The following classroom activity not only builds a positive classroom climate, but also demonstrates the importance and consequences of writing within a real context for communication. To prepare for this exercise, cut up a ream of paper (500 sheets) into fourths so that you will have 2,000 sheets of notepad-size paper. Bring these sheets into the classroom and give the following instructions to your students at the beginning of the period:

> "I want you to move to a part of the room where no one else is. Separate yourself from your classmates."

Once students have moved away from each other, make the following announcement:

> "Today there will be no talking in class. If you have anything to say to someone, write it down on this sheet [hand out one sheet to each student]. Write down your message; fold the sheet; address it by writing on the outside the recipient's name *and* your own name; then hold up your hand, and one of the messengers will come by, pick up your note, and give you another sheet for your next message."

Appoint two students to serve as "messengers" for this exercise.

That's all you need to say. The note writing begins, and you should participate in this exercise, also, writing notes for the entire period. You will be amazed at the amount of writing the students do. Usually, only two messengers are needed to pick up and deliver notes, but sometimes it is necessary to add a third because of all the note-writing activity. Besides building a positive classroom climate this way, I often get some valuable feedback from students. Sometimes I will write to students and ask, "Enjoying the class so far? What have you learned?" and get a good idea of their perception and understanding of the course content. Other times I will try to get students talking to others with whom they do not usually interact. For instance, write to one student and ask, "What does a wish look like?" and the reply usually comes back, "I don't know. What?" So send a second message: "I don't know, either. Why don't you write to Greg and Sarah and ask *them."* Soon, messages are being sent all over the room, each asking for an answer to the question of what a wish looks like.

The number of notes that are exchanged among students this way is incredible, and you will find the same result when you run the exercise in your own classroom. Why is there so much writing? And why is there so much enthusiasm among the students for this activity? One answer might be found in the *context* for this exercise—the conditions that are present during this communication experience. To explain, look first at the factors that surround our *oral* communication encounters. We speak when (1) we have something to say (or, at least, we *think* we have something to say); (2) there is an audience present (When was the last time you talked aloud to yourself?); and (3) we get feedback. When these three conditions exist together, we will talk. It is exactly the same with the note-writing activity. Notice that all three conditions (the context) are present: students are writing notes because they have something to say; they have a specific audience (they are writing their notes *to* someone); and they are able to obtain feedback quickly for their communication efforts.

When structuring writing assignments, then, you should be careful to provide for the presence and operation of these three conditions. In this way, students will write readily, enthusiastically, and with commitment.

Notes

1. Janet Emig provided the inspiration for the exercise on "What Does English Deal With?"

2. Portions of this discussion appeared in Golub (1988) and are used by permission of *Washington English Journal.*

3. Some of the potential topics in this list are suggested by or adapted from Leland and Mary Howe's *Personalizing Education* (1975, 209–10).

4. I've borrowed or adapted the names of these three principles from the Howes' book. Although I have not quoted from the authors' write-up of their "Positive Focus Game" (56–59), which they developed from Saville Sax's *Reality Games* (1972), I have adapted for my own classroom purposes their three principles of "focusing," "drawing out," and "acceptance," the third of which I call "listening without judging."

5. Two students, Steve and Odalys, have kindly volunteered to serve as models for this exercise. Odalys agreed to select a topic from the sheet and begin talking first, so Steve will be practicing the listening skills.

6. Brainstorming topics 3 and 6 are taken from Laliberte and Kehl (1969, n.p.).

Works Cited

Golub, Jeff. 1988. "What Does English Deal With?" *Washington English Journal* 2.1 (Fall): 47–49.

Howe, Leland W., and Mary Martha Howe. 1975. *Personalizing Education: Values, Clarification, and Beyond.* New York: Hart Publishing Company.

Johnston, Ellen Turlington [Ellen Johnston-Hale]. 1976. *We Don't Do Nothin' in Here.* With illustrations by Virginia and Sean McMahan. North Carolina: Moore Publishing Company. [Ellen T. Johnston-Hale's books are available from the author by writing to her at 942 White Rock Church Road, Chapel Hill, NC 27514.]

Laliberte, Norman, and Richey Kehl. 1969. *100 Ways to Have Fun with an Alligator and 100 Other Involving Art Projects.* N.P.: Art Education, Inc.

Renzulli, Joseph S. 1973. *New Directions in Creativity: Mark 2.* New York: Harper & Row.

Sax, Saville. 1972. *Reality Games.* New York: Popular Library.

Steiner, Claude. 1977. *The Original Warm Fuzzy Tale: A Fairytale.* With pictures by JoAnn Dick. Rolling Hills Estates, CA: Jalmar Press.

3 Establishing a Classroom Community and Context for Writing

Certain classroom procedures and principles of writing instruction should be established and discussed at the beginning of the course. Students need to know what it is that they will be doing and how they will be doing it. For instance, it is important to let students know about the kinds of writing involved and how this writing will be shared and evaluated in class. In addition, basic principles about the process of writing should be emphasized. In this chapter, then, I want to identify and describe certain points and procedures that work well to establish an interactive classroom community and context for writing.

The first point is that students will be writing for a *variety* of audiences and purposes. To concentrate on only *one kind* of writing is analogous to the idea of trying to teach someone to play the piano by having them practice only one key or note. Surely that student will arrive at a point where he or she can hit that key beautifully every time, but there is a lot more involved in mastering the instrument. The student must become adept at working with the *whole range* of keys and notes available if something musical and meaningful is to be achieved. In the same way, students need writing experiences that allow them to communicate across the whole range of discourse, so in this book you will find activities dealing with these kinds of writing and skills:

> creative writing
>
> personal experience narratives
>
> developing "voice" and "tone" in writing
>
> writing for a specific audience
>
> descriptive writing
>
> narrative writing
>
> persuasive writing
>
> character sketch
>
> comparison/contrast papers

writing about literature

research projects

Students also need to be made aware of how writing happens—of the various stages involved in the writing process. One of the problems that occurs frequently is that students tend to collapse the various stages into a one-shot writing effort. For instance, Jesse might try to write a rough draft of his paper in such a way that he can hand it in immediately upon completion as a polished final copy. So he will write the first three words, decide perhaps that this isn't quite how he wants to start out, and throw the paper away because he wants to begin again with a clean sheet. There is a way to help students overcome this problem of being concerned prematurely with "neatness" and "correctness" during their early drafting. Go to your local supermarket and persuade the management to give you several of those large, brown, grocery bags. Bring the bags to class, hand them out to your students, and tell them to do their initial drafting on those bags. Can you imagine trying to write *neatly* on a grocery bag? This technique might lead your students to abandon their premature concern with "neatness" and concentrate instead on *what* they want to say, getting their words out and moving language around in the process.

It is important, therefore, for students to see writing as a multi-step process. Even though some of the steps overlap or occur simultaneously (revising while drafting, for instance), students should come to see the different tasks and skills involved in completing a piece of writing. Their insights should include the points summarized in figure 1.

How Does Writing Happen?

Drafting: This is the initial stage of writing in which students simply get their ideas down on paper any way they can. It's a messy stage, as I mentioned before, but this is perfectly all right because that's how writing happens. Often, a student will bring me his or her rough draft to read and *apologize* because of all the crossed-out words and writing in the margins. I have to reassure the student in this case that it is normal and usual for drafts to appear this way. In looking at the draft, I ignore spelling and punctuation, concentrating instead on their clarity of thought and use of language. Why be concerned about this missing comma right now when the writer might eliminate that whole paragraph in a subsequent revision? Trying to *edit* a rough draft

---

How Does Writing Happen?

Four stages in the writing process:

1. Drafting
2. Revising
3. Editing
4. Polishing

Drafting stage

Four skills are involved in this stage:

1. Fluency—coming up with a lot of ideas to choose from.
2. Flexibility—looking at the topic in many different ways.
3. Originality—writing something different, unique, unusual.
4. Elaboration—adding details; giving an explanation.

Revising stage

Add a word, phrase, sentence, paragraph, or a whole new section to your paper.

Eliminate or take out something from your paper.

Change something around in your paper.

Substitute a word or phrase or sentence or section.

Editing stage

Check your writing for grammar and usage problems, spelling mistakes, and punctuation.

Polishing stage

To make a final copy of your paper, you should:

write on only one side of the paper;

have no mistakes in your spelling or punctuation.

Figure 1. Checklist of "Four Stages in the Writing Process."

is analogous to the act of pumping the brakes while the car is still in the garage!

Four creative thinking skills are needed during this drafting stage: fluency, flexibility, originality, and elaboration. "Fluency" is the ability to write easily and write a lot; "flexibility" involves being able to view something in different ways; "originality" is achieved when one comes up with something that is different, unique, unusual; and "elaboration" means adding appropriate details. Later in this chapter, I will describe activities that allow students to practice and develop these skills.

Revising: Much of writing involves *re*writing, and this is accomplished in one or more of these ways: by *adding* something (a word, a phrase, a sentence or a whole section); *eliminating* a part; *moving* something around (moving the second paragraph to the beginning of the paper, for instance); or *substituting* an item (by taking out this word or sentence and putting in something else). The revising process involves more than simply writing the draft over in ink. Let the students know exactly what is involved in revising. They need to understand that adding details or moving their writing around is a normal—and necessary—part of the process.

Editing: Once students have drafted their paper and revised it in response to feedback from their classmates, they are ready to *edit* it. This is assuming, of course, that they like what they have written and want to save it and make a final copy. *Now* it's time to "clean it up" by attending to the spelling and punctuation and other mechanical matters.

Polishing: The last step of the process is to make a "final copy" of the writing. In handing in this polished version or making it available for others to read, the student is declaring that "I am satisfied that this is the best I can do." The writing has been revised and edited extensively, and it is now ready for public presentation and evaluation. A final copy, then, should be prepared in such a way that it will make as favorable an impression as possible.

It may take some time for students to achieve a separation between their drafting and polishing efforts. Spending the first few weeks of writing instruction on drafting and revising only, however, will help students become more willing to take risks in their writing and worry less about editing concerns.

A second important principle of writing instruction is that *writing involves making choices—good writing is knowing the choices that are available to you.* Students need to be made aware of the choices they make throughout their writing. They choose a topic; decide what to say and how to say it; select from their repertoire of words. In revising, they look at other choices available, trying to determine other, perhaps even more effective, ways of saying what they want to say. One of the most important goals in writing instruction, then, is to expand students' awareness of the choices that are available to them in their writing, and a collaborative approach can be most helpful and effective here. By sharing their writing in small groups—by turning to their classmates for feedback—students learn about alternatives that might have escaped them otherwise. A simple exercise such as the following (based in part on Gerbrandt 1974, 55) can make this point clear to students.

Write the following words on the board and direct students to create as many sentences as they can with them. *All* of the words must be used in each sentence:

| dictionary | find | Mary | to | was |
| in | | told | word | the | the |

After ten minutes, ask for volunteers to read *one* of their sentence creations, instructing them to listen carefully so that they don't repeat a version that has already been read. You should find a surprising number of choices available here. There is the obvious combination, of course—

"Mary was told to find the word in the dictionary"

—which can be turned into a question:

"Was Mary told to find the word in the dictionary?"

But you can also identify the specific word that Mary had to find:

"Mary was to find the word 'told' in the dictionary."

Or you might use quotation marks to have Mary look up a different word:

"Find the word 'to' in the dictionary," Mary was told.

And the choices continue, more than ten of them, in fact—and my students are still coming up with new ones.

The point of this exercise becomes clear to students as they listen to their classmates' contributions. Each student has worked alone for 10 minutes moving those words around, trying to combine them in as many ways as possible. Perhaps the students found five or six different sentences and then stopped. That's all they could find. The possibilities ran out; no more choices were available to them. But then they hear sentence combinations they hadn't thought of. Groans of "Oh, no!" or cries of "Oh, yeah!" often accompany a student's reading of yet another combination that a classmate had not considered. And that's the point: students can do only so much alone, and then they must turn to someone else to learn about what other choices—in wording, in phrasing, in organization of one's writing —are available but as yet undiscovered and unconsidered. Sometimes ideas come from other people, and this exercise will help make that point clear to students.

Writing in Class

Most of the writing that students will do throughout the semester should be done in the classroom. By having students do their drafting in class, you are available to work with them and to respond to their initial ideas. In addition, students can also turn to their classmates at this time for ideas and feedback. The talk that students engage in during their drafting effort is an important part of the process of generating ideas, and you are providing the opportunity for this part of the process to occur.

You, as the teacher, should also write on the various topics and assignments right along with the students. This is probably *the most important way* to turn the classroom into a community of writers. Writing along with the students has several advantages: First, by working through the writing yourself, you are able to see the kinds of problems that the students are likely to encounter, either in understanding the demands of the task or in completing the assignment. Second, you can better judge the time needed to complete a draft since you are engaged in the drafting yourself. Third, since you will be asking students to share their writing orally with the rest of the class, you can model this practice by reading your own work. And finally—and most important—by writing on the topic yourself, you allow your students to see you as a *writer* as well as a teacher. It is one thing to tell the students about how "messy" the drafting process is; but let them see *your* rough draft with its crossed-out words and rephrasings and writing in the margins. Let them see your own struggle to write the first sentence and to find the right words. Whenever a student asks me to read his or her draft, I insist that, while I'm reading it, that the student reads *mine*. Often, while drafting with the class, I seek out one or more students and ask them for feedback or for help with a certain part of my writing. The students are surprised at first, but then *delighted* to be put in the role of *respondent* for the teacher's writing, to have their opinion sought and valued in this way. This is not just an act, either; I find that my students are able to read carefully and critically and to offer pertinent, valuable suggestions for revision.

Many of the examples of writing activities described in the following chapters are taken from the writing that I have done in class with my students.

Sharing Writing with the Whole Class

A strange thing happens when you stand in front of the class and announce that you want students to read aloud the writing they have just produced: students suddenly become fascinated with the top of their desks! At least, it appears this way because every head lowers as students stare at the woodgrain surface, hoping desperately that you won't call on *them* to read. It can be a threatening situation to be called upon to read one's own writing aloud, especially when the person called upon is either not ready to share (for whatever reason) or not confident about what he or she has drafted so far. The language and writing that a student produces is an extension of that student's self and so is tied to his or her self-image and esteem. It is important, therefore, that students be allowed to retain *control* of their writing.

One way to accomplish this is to establish a rule at the beginning of the course that any sharing of writing with the whole class will be done *on a volunteer basis only*. This rule contributes to a positive classroom climate by making students feel more comfortable and in control of their writing. There is a risk, of course, that *no one* will volunteer to read their writing aloud when the time comes for sharing. But this risk is still preferable to the discomfort generated by the practice of calling on students at random. Besides, there are ways to ensure that volunteers will come forth at the appropriate time. For instance, when the time comes to share rough drafts aloud with the whole class, you, the teacher, should read your writing *first*. The point is not to dare students to "try and top *this*," but rather to establish a climate for sharing. The attitude becomes one of "If I am asking you to share *your* writing, I should be willing to share *mine*." You are *modeling* behavior that you want students to imitate; once you finish reading your paper, you should find more than a few students willing to read *theirs*.

Another way to encourage students to volunteer a reading of their paper is to, in effect, *sign them up* in advance. As students individually show you their drafts, you might ask them privately if they would be willing to share their writing with the whole class when the time comes for oral readings. Several students will volunteer this way so that, when you are ready to have these papers read, you can simply call on them (since they volunteered in advance).

Once in a while, however, despite your best preparations and encouragement, you will find no volunteers at all when you ask for oral readings of drafts. You have just read your own paper aloud; you invite the next writer to read; and you simply get no response at all. Don't worry about it; it happens sometimes. Most importantly, *don't* violate your classroom rule and *call* on someone at random to break the silence. Imagine the message you would be communicating to the class through such a violation: "All public sharing of drafts will be done only through volunteering—unless there *are* no volunteers, in which case the rule doesn't count, and I will *make* you volunteer." There is a better way around this problem: if there are no volunteers to read aloud, simply wait a reasonable length of time and then direct students to *give* their writing to two classmates to read silently. The response will be immediate and enthusiastic. Students *want* to have an audience for their writing, remember. For some reason, the time or the nature of the assignment may not be quite right for an oral sharing at this moment. But almost every student will be willing to share his or her paper with two classmates and will eagerly read other papers to see what others have written. After this form of sharing, simply continue drafting or go on to the next activity. Perhaps later in the period—or the next day—you will have students volunteering when you ask.

Sharing Writing in Small Groups

Each paper the students write in class deserves an audience. Having students do their drafting without providing an audience for their effort is like asking students to speak into a "dead" telephone. No one talks into a telephone when there is no listener on the other end, and students won't enjoy writing when there is no one available to read their work. One way to provide an audience, as mentioned above, is to invite students to read their work aloud to the class. But not every student wants to participate in this manner; there is some risk involved, after all. So a suitable alternative is to have students share their drafts in small groups.

When the time comes to share rough drafts, direct students to assemble in small groups of 4 to 6 persons in each group. Each student in the group should read his or her paper aloud. After all papers have been read, the group should select *one* paper to be read aloud to the entire class, later in the period. The criteria for selection can vary depending on the nature of the topic being drafted. For instance, each group might select the paper that has the most unusual story line or the best introduction or the clearest description, etc.

After about 20 minutes of reading in small groups, the class reassembles and hears those drafts that were selected by each group. In this way, the members of each group get to hear the best papers of each of the other groups.

Handling the Paper Load

It is impossible to read every word (and every paper) the students write, especially in an English class in which a lot of writing occurs. But the students still need and deserve an audience for their writing. It's a problem, but there are some strategies we can use to keep the students writing frequently and to provide them with an audience without condemning ourselves to reading fifty or more papers each night.

Encourage students to be an audience for each other's writing efforts, both in small groups and as a whole class. I follow the procedures described above for the sharing of students' papers and then collect the drafts and give the students credit for having had their paper ready for reading by the deadline. But I won't read the papers and write individual responses at this time—I don't have to. The students have been provided with a considerable (and appreciative) audience, already. Moreover, because we do much of our drafting in class, I have already read and commented on many of these papers, and my responses were given in an individual face-to-face conference with the student. This is probably the best time to confer with the students on their writing, at an early stage while they are still working on their papers. Once they have completed their papers, they are less open to suggestions for change and improvement.

Not every paper needs to be revised and made into a final copy. Sometimes it is enough simply to have students try a particular kind of writing and share their "rough-draft" thoughts. And not every assignment will work out for the students. Requiring that every paper be made into a final copy and graded has the effect of reducing students' willingness to take risks in their writing—better to "play it safe" and write what the teacher wants if it's going to be evaluated for a grade.

To encourage risk taking and at the same time increase the amount of writing that students do, I try to give students control over which drafts they submit for evaluation and a grade. During a creative writing unit, for instance, the students will draft on three or four topics, but only one of the papers (students' choice) is selected for extensive revision and submission as a final copy. Each of the drafts is written in class and shared in small groups. But not all of the drafts will work out, so not all of them should be revised and graded. By letting students know ahead of time that they will have this choice available to them, I encourage them to take risks in their writing. The message is clear: "It's okay if a paper doesn't work out as well as you would like." I try to follow this procedure when engaging students in a variety of writing tasks. If we are producing a comparison/contrast essay, for example, I will have students draft on three or four topics, share them in small groups, then select one of those papers for revision and submission as a final copy. This procedure also helps control the paper load—the students do a lot of writing without the teacher having to read everything they write. Yet, the use of small groups still allows students to have the audience they need for their writing efforts.

Another way to control the paper load is to have students work in pairs to produce a draft. There is a tremendous amount of student talking that occurs—but it is productive talk—as students work together to decide what to say and how to say it. Such an arrangement engages students in the construction and negotiation of meanings, and this process is at the heart of what it means to "do English." In pairs, students try out their ideas on each other, modifying and shaping their responses in accordance with the feedback they receive from each other. And a second benefit of this paired arrangement is that it cuts the teacher's paper load in half. Sometimes I will have students work in pairs to answer a question about a piece of literature under discussion, but I will hand out 3 x 5 index cards to each pair and direct students to write their final response on the card. This is another way to control the paper load: students must be concise in their response if they are to fit their answer on the card. Writing concisely is certainly a worthwhile skill for students to practice. And it makes for a lot less reading for the teacher.

Evaluating Writing

What about the *criteria* for evaluation of students' final copies? For many kinds of writing, there are three standards that always seem appropriate and worthwhile, and these criteria should be made known to the students from the very beginning of their drafting efforts. The writing should be

1. *Clear.* You should be able to understand what it is the student is trying to say and the points that the student is trying to make.

2. *Complete.* The student has provided sufficient details to allow you to understand the situation or problem being presented.

3. *Convincing.* This criterion is especially appropriate for persuasive writing in which the student is trying to present his or her position on an issue. Even if you disagree with the student's point of view, you should find a strong case presented with some valid arguments and evidence used.

Other criteria might be appropriate for a particular kind of writing only, and these standards, once again, should be made clear at the time the assignment is given. How can students aim for a "good" piece of writing if they don't know what the criteria for "goodness" are?

Another way to establish the criteria for a particular piece of writing is to allow the students to set forth the standards themselves. Once their final copies have been handed in, the students should spend time in class generating the criteria that you, the teacher, will use in evaluating those papers. This can be a risky approach, however—you must be willing to *use* the criteria that the students create. If you are going to play a "game" with the students in which you *pretend* to solicit their suggestions, but afterward go ahead and, in the end, use your *own* criteria anyway, then it is better to publicize your own criteria from the beginning and skip this approach. Otherwise, you are being dishonest, and the students will catch on quickly to this 'game,' declining to participate sincerely and actively in the future when you once again ask for their input. But if you do ask your students to generate appropriate criteria—and convince them that *you will, indeed, use their suggestions*—then you should find that they will work (and think and discuss) hard to create pertinent, worthwhile standards that can be applied in your evaluation. And they will have learned a lot in the process, not only about what constitutes a "good" piece of writing, but also about how well their own writing came to meeting these standards that they established themselves.

Summary

Because writing involves making choices, the aim of writing instruction is to expand the repertoire of choices available to the students.

One way to achieve this goal is to have students turn to their class-mates at all stages of the writing process for responses and sugges-tions. In this way, students learn of choices for their writing that they might not have considered previously.

Students deserve to have an audience for their writing, and small-group work is an excellent way to provide that audience. All drafts should be shared, either in small groups or with the whole class on a volunteer basis only. But not all drafts need to be revised and edited into a final copy. Allow the *students* to decide which of their papers to fix up for final evaluation and grading. They will feel more in control of their writing because they are the ones who select which paper will represent their best work. This approach will also ease the paper load for you because you do not need to evaluate every piece of writing for a grade. Working with the students in class as they draft and share and revise will enable you to monitor their writing suffi-ciently; in addition, it is *while* the students are drafting that they are most open to suggestions for improvement. Once the paper is made into a final copy, further suggestions will have little impact.

Work Cited

Gerbrandt, Gary L. 1974. *An Idea Book for Acting Out and Writing Language, K–8.* Urbana: National Council of Teachers of English.

4 Creative Writing Activities

The writing activities described in this chapter provide opportunities for students to write for a variety of audiences and purposes. Some of the descriptions are accompanied by prewriting suggestions and ideas for sharing and revising the drafts that the students produce. As a reminder, the following conditions, if maintained when working with these topics, will turn the classroom into an interactive writing community:

1. Provide an audience for the students' drafts. Whether sharing drafts through volunteers reading aloud to the rest of the class or moving students into small groups, make sure that the students' writing is exposed to an audience at some point in the process.

2. Write your own draft as the students are working on theirs. Working on your own draft will change your relationship with your students, making you a colleague, a fellow writer, one who is also struggling with, and experiencing, the same demands of the task at hand. In addition, by reading your own writing aloud, you encourage students to read theirs through your modeling behavior. To reinforce this point, I have used my own drafts produced in class as examples for several of the writing activities presented below.

3. Focus on the choices available to students at various stages of their writing. Encourage students to show their writing to their classmates as a way to find out what works and what *doesn't* work in their writing. Classmates can point out other ways of saying something or places where clarification or elaboration is needed. A cooperative atmosphere, therefore, should be emphasized throughout the writing and revising process so that students will be more likely to turn to each other for this kind of help.

DEVELOPING STUDENTS' CREATIVE THINKING SKILLS

The first few weeks in class should be spent simply drafting on different kinds of topics, developing students' fluency, flexibility, originality, and elaboration skills. Have students share their writing, but leave it in draft form. This is a time for students to learn to take risks, cross out words and phrases and sections, write fast and messy. Go for the good ideas and leave matters of correctness and neatness for later.

Developing Fluency

"Tell Lies"

> "You can write this paper as a poem, a letter, a story, a newspaper article—in whatever form you want. But you must tell lies—everything you say must be a lie."

This topic invites students to consider outrageous possibilities. Students usually have no trouble coming up with an idea and beginning to write immediately. Sometimes I will have students draft *twice* on this topic. After the first draft is completed, we'll share what we have, listen to each other's papers to learn of choices for topics we hadn't considered, and then draft a second time. The second papers are almost always more imaginative than the first attempts. This topic gets students started drafting immediately and allows them to use their imagination and begin considering possibilities.

The Third Eye

> "Everyone has *three* eyes. Two of your eyes see everything *without*, and one eye—the *third* one—sees everything *within*. This activity will allow you to *see* with that 'third eye.' I want you to imagine that you are in a movie theater. Imagine also that the music I'm going to play for you now is the *soundtrack* of the film you are watching. As you listen to the music, write down—as fast as you can—what you see happening on the screen."

For this exercise, I use classical music that is unusually expressive and "moody": "The Sorcerer's Apprentice" (by Ducas), "The Planets" (Holst), and "Scheherazade" (Rimsky-Korsakov) work well here, but there are others, I'm sure, that would work equally as well. Encourage students to write *constantly* as the music plays. If their "movie" should suddenly change from a western to a space fantasy, that's fine. "Just start writing about the fantasy and keep going." When the music ends, you should find that many students have written as much as two to three pages. Ask for volunteers to summarize what their movie was about, and then direct students to show their paper to two classmates so that all will have had an audience for their effort.

You might even repeat this exercise with different music the next day or a week later. I found a variation that the students also like. I bring in Mussorgsky's composition "Pictures at an Exhibition" and tell the class that the composer wrote this music in response to some of the paintings he saw in a museum. The music is composed of separate sections, each section linked by a common musical theme that represents the composer's walking from one picture to another in the museum: "As I play each of the different pieces of music that represent different pictures, write about what you think the picture is showing."

This exercise gets the students writing fluently without being overly concerned with matters of "correctness."

Developing Flexibility

"Flexibility" involves the ability to see an object or a situation in different ways, and these writing activities can help students become more flexible in their perception. They must adopt, and see something from, another point of view.

Object Obituaries

This idea comes from the NCTE publication *Ideas for Teaching English in the Junior High and Middle School* (Carter and Rashkis 1980). It's a wonderful resource, full of practical, clever, innovative activities. This is one of them:

> The obituary column is a regular feature in nearly every newspaper in the United States. Its purpose is to give pertinent information about people who have died recently. Some newspapers take a flowery approach ("beloved cousin of Rachel, Susan, and James"); others adopt a more objective tone. (234)

Read one or two sample obituaries from your local newspaper, and then tell students to write one of their own. But the obituary they write will be about an *object* and should include the following pertinent information:

> how the object died
>
> how old it was
>
> what the object accomplished in life
>
> where the object lived
>
> survivors of the object
>
> funeral arrangements (234)

So the students might write about Peter Pencil, for instance, who lived (where else?) in Pennsylvania (sorry about that). Here are a couple of other examples to get you and your students started:

Bobby Bagboy, 15, died today after being crushed to death in a wastebasket. Bobby, a shopping bag at the local Buy-'n-Belch Food Store, had been a solid member of our community for more than a week. He distinguished himself by once carrying 5 cantaloupes, 8 soup cans, 15 packages of Rice-a-Roni, and a watermelon—all without spilling or tearing.

His survivors include his 4 little baggies and his brother, Glad. The funeral will be held at the Buy-'n-Belch Memorial Incinerator at 2:00 PM tomorrow where Bobby will make an ash of himself.

Cindy Circuit-Breaker was electrocuted this morning when her owner accidentally overloaded her wires. This shocking incident occurred just after the coffee began perking, the toaster was plugged in, and the dishwasher was run. Things really began to heat up when Cindy's owner decided to shave with his electric razor. At that moment, Cindy got watts she deserved, and she melted away in despair.

For years Cindy had run the household with energy and enthusiasm. Sometimes, however, she was a troublemaker and often got the children in hot water, especially during their baths.

Wire services will be held next Monday.

Encourage students to experiment with puns and clever phrases and unusual happenings for their object. And encourage two or more students to work together on a draft, too. Some of the best ideas happen that way.

Object Talking

"Imagine that you are an object talking to either another object or to a human. Perhaps you are complaining about something or sharing an incident that happened to you. Write what you would say to this audience."

When I first started using this topic, I structured it as "A Day in the Life of . . . (a locker, a pencil, etc.)." But without provision for an *audience*, the writing lacked sparkle and imagination. By specifying that the object should be talking *to* something or someone else, I got better results. Here are some examples:

"Hey, you! Yeah, you who think it's so neat to carry me around from class to class, impressing your friends with how much work you have to do. You know, the teacher checked me out to you for a reason: you're supposed to be *reading* my pages, not writing on them. Have you even looked at my story on page 42? I think you'd like it. You like motorcycles? I've got 'em on page 98. How about rock stars? I've got those, too. You really should be reading me. I've got a lot to tell you.

"But whether you read me or not, you'd better stop mistreating me. I don't like what you said about the teacher on page 12, and you better get your gum out of my Table of Contents, or I'm telling on you."

"I beg your pardon, dear child, but you have been playing that same wretched passage for the last 10 minutes, and you *still* haven't gotten it right. Is it *my* fault, perhaps? Are my keys too large for your teensy-tiny little fingers? Or maybe it's that I hide the *one* black key you need when it's time to play the fourth note that you're always missing.

"I'm sure that you can't be having all this trouble simply because you haven't practiced on my keyboard for the past 3 weeks. No, that can't be it. And certainly the rancid sounds coming from my badly-warped strings are not due to the lemonade you spilled all over me yesterday."

Developing Originality

Telling Tall Tales

Telling "tall tales" is a good way to stretch one's imagination and reach for something different, unique, unusual. Following is a variation on the traditional tall tale that I discovered at an English conference.[1]

Give students a copy of the handout, "Telling Tall Tales" (figure 1). Read one of the story starters aloud to give students a sense of the kind of writing involved here, writing that invites students to tell an outrageously exaggerated story. Each story starter requires a specific example of just how "tiny" or "fast" or "pretty" the turkey was. Here are some examples from one of my classes:

> There was no doubt about it! Tabitha Turkey was an unusually pretty turkey. I mean, there are ugly turkeys and ordinary-looking turkeys and good-looking turkeys, and then there was Tabitha. Pretty. That was the only word to describe her. In fact, she was so pretty that . . .

> . . . word of her beauty spread quickly throughout all Turkeydom. This caused quite a problem, especially around the time of the annual Turkey Tango and Drumstick Dinner Dance. This affair occurred just one week prior to Thanksgiving, and it was a problem because all the turkeys in the country flocked to Tabitha's farm in hopes of catching a glimpse of her bright feathers or her shapely drumsticks. Shoppers at Safeway and ladies at Lucky's looked aghast as all the turkeys on the grocer's shelves rolled out the doors and scrambled to hitch a ride to Tabitha's place. Feathers flew as all the turkeys in the world gobbled and galloped their way across miles of deserts and

Telling Tall Tales

Tom Turkey was a big turkey. Now, I don't mean an ordinary big turkey. No, Sir! I mean an extraordinary, gigantic big turkey. In fact, Tom Turkey was so big that . . .

Terrence Turkey's hearing was so keen that he could hear a flea sneeze at forty paces. Now, that means he could hear just about anything that was said or done anywhere in the barnyard. As you might imagine, this unusual ability caused some problems for Terrence. In fact, I remember one day when . . .

There was no doubt about it! Tabitha Turkey was an unusually pretty turkey. I mean, there are ugly turkeys and ordinary-looking turkeys and good-looking turkeys, and then there was Tabitha. Pretty. That was the only word to describe her. In fact, she was so pretty that . . .

As turkeys go, Terrell Turkey was slow. He just couldn't seem to do anything any faster than a snail's pace. He ate slowly. He thought slowly, and he walked slowly. In fact, Terrell was so slow that when he crossed the road, it took him two days to reach the other side. Now, this caused Terrell some problems. In fact, I remember one day when Terrell . . .

Tanya Turkey was absolutely tiny. Her mother was worried. Her father was worried. Even her grandparents were worried and so were her aunts and uncles. Tanya had been eating as much as she could at each and every meal for as long as she could remember, but she was still tiny. In fact, she was so tiny that the other turkeys were always stepping on her and bumping into her because they could scarcely see her, and when she turned sideways, she would practically disappear. Now, one day . . .

Tony Turkey was strong—so strong that she could lick any turkey in the yard and lift anything around. In fact, she was so strong that no one knew exactly how strong she was. They were afraid to ask and couldn't think of any safe way to measure. One day, however, circumstances put Tony's strength to the test. It was a warm, sunny day and . . .

Figure 1. "Telling Tall Turkey Tales" story starters.

forests and rivers and ranches—all seeking Tabitha's wing in marriage.

Well, this just couldn't go on any longer. Last year's Dance-o-Thon, the "Turkey Gravy Gallop and Ruffled Feather Wing Fling," caused a stampede as all that white meat on the hoof, so to speak, jostled for position next to Tabitha.

Farmers and grocers alike agreed that something had to be done. So this year the owner of Tabitha's farm decided to hold a special roast at which Tabitha would be the guest of honor: beautiful Tabitha was lured to the chopping block by the owner's son who flattered her with his praise of her pretty giblets. He spoke to her of all the unnatural things he'd like to do to her wishbone and . . . well, wouldn't *you* be taken in by such compliments?

Within minutes Tabitha became a changed turkey: she received a split personality, turned a golden-brown and sat at the place of honor on the owner's table. All the members of the owner's family agreed that Tabitha was indeed pretty: she was pretty tender and pretty good-tasting.

All of Tabitha's fans and followers, known locally as the Gravy Groupies, decided suddenly that maybe being pretty wasn't all it was cooked *up* to be.

Tony Turkey was strong—so strong that she could lick any turkey in the yard and lift anything around. In fact, she was so strong that no one knew exactly how strong she was. They were afraid to ask and couldn't think of any safe way to measure. One day, however, circumstances put Tony's strength to the test. It was a warm, sunny day and . . .

. . . a family from the city arrived at Tony's farm to buy a turkey for their Thanksgiving dinner. Wouldn't you know it? They picked out Tony for their feast and paid the owner immediately.

Getting Tony into the car, however, was only the first of their problems. Just as soon as Tony realized that she had been invited to dinner at this family's home, she strutted over to their car and kicked a hole in their door. But the family was persistent and, pushing and shoving, they forced Tony into the back seat.

What a mistake! They hadn't been on the freeway ten minutes when Tony decided suddenly that she had had enough: she slammed her feet through the floor of the back seat and brought the whole car to a sliding halt. Then, standing up inside the car, Tony turned around and headed *up* the freeway, back the way she had come, dodging traffic expertly, all the while wearing the car around her like a life preserver. Other drivers barely avoided skidding off the road into a ditch as they gawked at this one car that appeared to be equipped, not with four wheels, but with turkey feet.

So now when people ask you: "What was Tony doing on the freeway last week?" You can tell them: "Oh, about 35 M.P.H."

Have students read their drafts in small groups, asking each group to select *one* paper to be read aloud to the class. The criteria for selection should be a paper that is different, unique, and unusual.

Developing Elaboration

Twisted Fairy Tales

This exercise involves students in writing parodies of familiar fairy tales. You might, for example, read from the book *Revolting Rhymes* by

Roald Dahl (1982) as either an introduction or a follow-up to this activity:

1. Brainstorm as a class all the titles of fairy tales that come to mind. Write them on the board or overhead projector.

2. Ask students to work in pairs and list all the "common elements" or ingredients of fairy tales (many contain giants, castles, magic, a dragon, a prince or princess, a forest, a happy ending, etc.).

3. Have the students, still working in pairs, select *one* particular fairy tale and circle those items on the list they have just made that appear in their story.

4. Then direct students to "*change* two of those items in your fairy tale, and then re-write the story. For instance, let's say that the magic beans in 'Jack and the Beanstalk' did not give rise to a beanstalk but to something else; and let's say that the giant did not live in a castle in the air but instead hid out in an abandoned warehouse. Make those changes as you rewrite the story. What else will have to change in your retelling?"

Some clever revisions of the original fairy tales should result as students find that the two changes they have created affect the story in significant ways. It is quite a skill to retell the story in a way that incorporates—and is consistent with—those changes.

The writing activities described above are especially appropriate to use at the beginning of the course. They invite students to take risks, write fast, and see things in new and different ways. In addition, you can use the initial drafts as a vehicle for establishing and demonstrating the procedures the students will follow throughout the semester in sharing their work in small groups. The skills and approach to writing that the students practice here will be used in all of their subsequent writing efforts.

WRITING FROM PERSONAL EXPERIENCE

Personal experience essays and narratives and poems offer students adventures in writing, opportunities to apply what they have learned from their playing with language in the previous creative writing activities. Their developing fluency, flexibility in thinking, and ability to elaborate will serve students well as they turn their attention to the more serious task of capturing personal experiences in writing.

Remembering an Incident

"Write about remembering a particular incident—an incident that is hard to forget."[2]

To introduce this topic, I read the following passage from Dick Gregory's (1964) autobiography as a model of personal experience writing. Dick Gregory is an African American comedian and social activist who, in this excerpt, relates a memorable, painful childhood incident that happened to him at school. This writing affects the reader through its dialogue and telling details:

> I never learned hate at home, or shame. I had to go to school for that. I was about seven years old when I got my first big lesson. I was in love with a little girl named Helene Tucker, a light-complexioned little girl with pigtails and nice manners. She was always clean and she was smart in school. I think I went to school then mostly to look at her. . . .
>
> I guess I would have gotten over Helene by summertime, but something happened in that classroom that made her face hang in front of me for the next twenty-two years. . . .
>
> It was on a Thursday. I was sitting in the back of the room in a seat with a chalk circle drawn around it. The idiot's seat, the troublemaker's seat.
>
> The teacher thought I was stupid. Couldn't spell, couldn't read, couldn't do arithmetic. Just stupid. Teachers were never interested in finding out that you couldn't concentrate because you were so hungry, because you hadn't had any breakfast. All you could think about was noontime, would it ever come? Maybe you could sneak into the cloakroom and steal a bite of some kid's lunch out of a coat pocket. A bite of something. Paste. You can't really make a meal of paste, or put it on bread for a sandwich, but sometimes I'd scoop a few spoonfuls out of the paste jar in the back of the room. . . . Paste doesn't taste too bad when you're hungry.
>
> The teacher thought I was a troublemaker. All she saw from the front of the room was a little black boy who squirmed in his idiot's seat and made noises and poked the kids around him. I guess she couldn't see a kid who made noises because he wanted someone to know he was there.
>
> It was on a Thursday, the day before the Negro payday. The eagle always flew on Friday. The teacher was asking each student how much his father would give to the Community Chest.

On Friday night, each kid would get the money from his father, and on Monday he would bring it to the school. I decided I was going to buy me a Daddy right then. I had money in my pocket from shining shoes and selling papers, and whatever Helene Tucker pledged for her Daddy I was going to top it. And I'd hand the money right in. I wasn't going to wait until Monday to buy me a Daddy.

I was shaking, scared to death. The teacher opened her book and started calling out names alphabetically.

"Helene Tucker?"

"My Daddy said he'd give two dollars and fifty cents."

"That's very nice, Helene. Very, very nice indeed."

That made me feel pretty good. It wouldn't take too much to top that. I had almost three dollars in dimes and quarters in my pocket. I stuck my hand in my pocket and held onto the money, waiting for her to call my name. But the teacher closed her book after she called everybody else in the class.

I stood up and raised my hand.

"What is it now?"

"You forgot me."

She turned toward the blackboard. "I don't have time to be playing with you, Richard."

"My Daddy said he'd . . ."

"Sit down, Richard, you're disturbing the class."

"My Daddy said he'd give . . . fifteen dollars."

She turned around and looked mad. "We are collecting this money for you and your kind, Richard Gregory. If your Daddy can give fifteen dollars you have no business being on relief."

"I got it right now, I got it right now, my Daddy gave it to me to turn in today, my Daddy said . . ."

"And furthermore," she said, looking right at me, her nostrils getting big and her lips getting thin and her eyes opening wide, "We know you don't have a Daddy."

Helene Tucker turned around, her eyes full of tears. She felt sorry for me. Then I couldn't see her too well because I was crying, too.

"Sit down, Richard."

And I always thought the teacher kind of liked me. She always picked me to wash the blackboard on Friday, after school. That was a big thrill, it made me feel important. If I didn't wash it, come Monday the school might not function right.

"Where are you going, Richard?"

I walked out of school that day, and for a long time I didn't go back very often. There was shame there. (44–46)

This is a powerful piece of writing, and it affects my students every time I read it aloud. The students can *feel* the pain, the disappointment, the humiliation. This is what writing from personal experience can do. Other appropriate examples and models for personal experience writing may be found in student texts and anthologies.

In preparation for writing their own personal experience paper, students identify the characteristics of the above passage that indeed make it an outstanding piece of writing. Certainly the incident is one that is, for the author, hard to forget. And then there is the use of dialogue and pertinent details that makes the incident come alive for the reader. But, there is something more: in the above passage, the author has focused on *a very specific, sharply defined incident.* It is an experience that had a definite beginning and ending. This is an important point to emphasize to students. In selecting their own personal experience to write about, students should choose an incident that occurred, for instance, between 10:13 and 10:17 a.m. It might take a paragraph or two to explain the prior events or circumstances leading up to the specific incident being described, but the event itself should be one that happened fairly quickly within a short span of time.

The reason for emphasizing this point is that students sometimes choose for their personal experience, not a specific incident, but instead a certain extended time period involving a *series* of events. Their writing, then, becomes fuzzy and vague, sounding more like a series of diary entries. Imagine, for instance, reading a student's personal experience paper that begins: "Last summer I spent a month at basketball camp. It was great! During the first week, we. . . ." You will probably encounter a whole string of stories, none of which will be told in much detail. Better to suggest to students in advance that they select a personal experience for their writing that has a sharply defined beginning and ending, and that occurred at a specific point in time. In this way, the focus will be clear and constant. Following is an example of a personal experience of my own:

Sledding Accident Is a Big Hit with Scout

My years in the Boy Scouts were memorable mainly because of the camping trips we went on. The memory of *one* of these trips, in fact, stays with me today, in the form of a two-inch scar on my leg.

We were staying in a lodge at Big Bear Lake, a camping spot in Northern California. The entire area was covered with snow and the nearby hill was *made* for sledding.

Had to be careful, however, when steering the sled. The trick was to get up speed quickly, then turn hard at the bend in the road; otherwise, you'd continue down the hill and into the lake at the bottom.

Because the kids at the beginning or top of the hill could not see around the bend, we had a scout stationed at an appropriate spot to yell to us when the lower half of the road (after the turn) was clear.

My turn to sled. Oh, joy! Jump on the sled, yell to the spotter, "All clear?"

"Oh, yeah!!" came the reply.

Shoot down the top half, turn hard—Oh, good! I won't be going into the lake *this* time!—get set for the best part of the ride . . . .

And then I saw him—a scout perched on his sled right in the middle of the road. By the time he saw me, he could look straight up at me because my sled simply slid right over him. Didn't hurt him a bit. But *my* sled came to a stop a little before *I* did, and thus the two-inch scar on my leg. It seems I got more than I tobogganed for!

After completing their rough drafts of this essay—but before moving into small groups to read their writing aloud—students might review criteria for a "good" personal experience paper. In this way, students will be prepared to listen critically and carefully as their classmates read, and they will also gain some valuable insight into the quality of their *own* draft.

Childhood Game

"Write about what it was like playing a childhood game."[3]

This topic invites students to reach way back into their memories and re-capture a moment. Several students may choose to write this piece as a poem. That's what I did the first time I tried it:

Moving across the field—
crouching, creeping, watching out for others—
We hunted and waited for our chance to "Capture the Flag."
This was war! One wrong step in the wrong direction—
an unwary motion—
And our world of play was shattered.
I *still* watch my step. I *still* make no unwary motions.

I *still* watch out for others.
But I'm not playing anymore.

It's not a game! Why do you call it a "game"? It's not a game when I can't run fast enough and so the ref calls me "out" at first base. That's a game? Lot of fun *that* is when I have to walk all the way back to the bench and everyone's staring at me and thinking, "Why'd the coach have to put him on OUR team?"

And I don't think that "Monopoly" is really a game, either. Everyone else lands on the good spots and buys all those cards with the colors and I only get that stupid card with the lightbulb on it or else I have to go to jail and miss my turn for 3 years.

Games are supposed to be fun. You're supposed to *win* when you play a game. Guess I never thought that in order for someone to win, someone else has to lose. That's okay, I guess. It's only a game. . . .

But why does it always have to be ME?

Notes

1. The source for this exercise is unknown to me. If any readers know its origins, please contact the publisher so that appropriate documentation can be included in this chapter.

2. The source of this quote is Jacobs (1976, 6).

3. The "Childhood Game" topic is taken from Jacobs (1976, 6).

Works Cited

Carter, Candy, and Zora M. Rashkis, eds. 1980. *Ideas for Teaching English in the Junior High and Middle School.* Urbana: National Council of Teachers of English.

Dahl, Roald. 1982. *Roald Dahl's Revolting Rhymes.* New York: Knopf.

Jacobs, Lucky. 1976. "Creative Writing Assignments Based on Basic Processes." Paper presented at the Annual Convention of the Conference on College Composition and Communication. Philadelphia. 25–27 March. ERIC: ED 127 623.

Gregory, Dick, with Robert Lipsyte. 1964. *Nigger: An Autobiography.* New York: E. P. Dutton.

5 Descriptive Writing Activities

Good descriptive writing works because of the writer's use of appropriate, fresh, vivid words and images. By appealing to the various senses, and by creating "word pictures," the writer brings to life a scene or a situation. The activities in this section, then, work to develop students' descriptive writing skills. The first exercises presented below allow students to play with language and engage their imagination. The more formal compositions follow and build on the skills developed by the initial wordplay. Throughout these activities, students should share their responses with each other so that they can hear new ideas and learn about other choices for their writing.

Synesthesia

This activity allows students to play with words and consider unusual possibilities and combinations of ideas.[1] Ask students to write down several words and phrases in response to the following three questions. After each question is asked, allow time for students to write their responses; then call on volunteers to share what they have written before going on to the next question.

1. "What does a fire-engine siren *sound* like?" (piercing, screeching; like the sound of a baby screaming, etc.)
2. "What does the bark of a tree *feel* like?" (rough, scratchy, prickly; feels like sandpaper, etc.)
3. "What does laughter *taste* like?"

Expect an uproar from the class: "Wait a minute! You can't *taste* laughter! You can *hear* a siren and you can *feel* tree bark, but you can't taste laughter. That's silly; it's impossible!" The first time I tried this exercise, I encountered a babble of confused, complaining voices at this question, and then, in the midst of the noise, a voice at the back of the room yelled, "Oh, I get it! It tastes like the fizz on a Coke!" Sudden silence, and then a couple of other contributions were offered. And the minds were opened.

The first two questions are "normal" in that they deal with only one *sense*. We *expect* to hear sirens and feel bark. But the third question *combines* two senses and so requires a leap of imagination: "Of course you can't taste laughter—but *if* you could, what would it taste like?"

Once students have made this imaginary leap into the world of combined senses, changing a sound into a taste, they are ready for more examples such as the following:

"What does the color green feel like?"

"What does a sparkle taste like?"

"What does pain look like?"

"What does a cloud feel like?"

Follow up these kinds of questions with ones that deal with abstract qualities and concepts:

"What does a wish look like?" (One student wrote in response to this question: ". . . like a balloon being slowly filled with air.")

"What does sadness smell like?"

"What does an idea look like?"

"What does anger taste like?

"What does thunder look like?"

Begin asking questions, too, that call for comparisons between two seemingly disparate things, one of which is "normal" or expected and the other abstract:

"Which is softer, velvet or a whisper?"

"Which is more painful, a broken finger or a broken heart?"

"Which is higher, the clouds in the sky or a person's hopes and dreams?"

"Which is taller, a giraffe or an unhappy feeling?"

"Which is deeper, a hole or a secret?"

You can go on to ask some really strange questions:

"Which is slower, 'K' or 'Z'?"

"Which is louder, a closed book or an open book?"

"Which is happier, a door or a window?"

"Which tastes better, a number or a letter?"

Once you have come this far, *anything* is possible:

"How long is forever?"

"Where do you go when you're asleep?"

> "What do birds do on their day off?"
>
> "What do mirrors think of us?"
>
> "How many feathers does it take to fly?"
>
> "What happens to your words after you speak them?"
>
> "How did the monsters get into your closet?"
>
> "If you were a piece of paper, and a pencil were writing on you, what would it feel like?"

After sharing responses to some of these kinds of questions, invite students to create similar questions of their own. Read some of them aloud in class; have students generate answers to their classmates' questions; and post the best, most provocative and imaginative questions on the classroom walls. Buy or make some "sentence strips," long, narrow strips of heavy construction paper, and write the students' questions on them. They'll be a constant, vivid reminder of what can happen when one plays with impossible possibilities.

"Happiness is . . ."

Charles Schulz, creator of the popular "Peanuts" comic strip, wrote and illustrated a book, *Happiness Is a Warm Puppy* (1962), in which he offers several "word pictures" to illustrate and exemplify the abstract quality of "happiness." You can't see "happiness." You can't go into the supermarket and purchase two pounds or three quarts of "happiness." But you *can* visualize it through a concrete image, something you can see or hear or taste or feel—thus the word picture of happiness being "a warm puppy." I read some of Schulz's word pictures and then invite students to create their own, for example:

> Happiness is . . . getting all your homework done and still having an hour left to make chocolate chip cookies before bedtime.
>
> Happiness is . . . getting the phone number of the girl you like who sits two rows in front of you in class.

For those students who might have trouble with this exercise, I tell them to imagine that they are holding in their hand a postcard that shows a photograph of "happiness": "What do you see on this postcard? What is this a picture *of*? Now describe that picture in words."

After sharing responses, we go on to create word pictures of *other* abstract qualities such as loneliness, anger, love, fear, winter. One student wrote, "Loneliness is . . . the last tree in the lot on Christmas

Eve," and another student pictured loneliness as "an empty mailbox." But one of the most powerful word pictures I have ever read was created by a student of mine several years ago who, for some reason, did not participate in any class activities at all except this one, when he wrote, "Peace is . . . when there's no more ammunition left."

Creating Expressed Comparisons

Another way to create word pictures is through similes or expressed comparisons. Direct the students to complete one or more of the following phrases, trying for images that are different, unique, unusual:

> as funny as . . .
>
> as frightened as . . .
>
> as tired as . . .
>
> as nervous as . . .

Encourage students to generate their *own* comparisons as a follow-up activity ("as quick as . . .", "as silly as . . .", etc.) and then complete their phrases with word pictures.

Word Banks

A common exercise during a descriptive writing unit is to brainstorm lists of words that appeal to the various senses. A "word bank" is created this way—lists of "sight" words and "sound" words and words that describe the sense of "taste," etc.—that one can draw upon as one writes a descriptive paper. Certainly, this is a worthwhile activity, but it doesn't have to stop there. Following are some other word banks that students might create.

Onomatopoeia

Ask students to copy down some of the following words as you write them on the board. By the time you finish writing your fourth or fifth word, you will hear students calling out their own contributions to your growing list on the board:

plump	clink	plop	tap	buzz
crash	hiss	crackle	boom	snap
sizzle	slurp	bloop	chomp	crunch

These are onomatopoeic words—words that sound like what they mean—and students can generate a tremendous list in a short time.

Once they have compiled a fairly sizable word bank, direct them to draw upon it to describe some of these sounds:

the sound of a thunderstorm

wind blowing through the trees

a person walking through mud

glass breaking

water dripping from a faucet

logs burning in a fireplace

people eating potato chips

After sharing responses, have students put this list away. They'll have occasion to refer to it later, and it will serve as a nice resource for their descriptive writing.

"Get out of here!" she (said).

Too often, students will settle for the first word they think of instead of going one step further and looking at other, perhaps more descriptive, word choices available to them. This next word bank will help make them aware of one such wide array of choices.

Write this sentence on the board: "Get out of here!" she (*said*). Start writing a list of alternative words for that space: "whispered," "screeched," "muttered," etc. The students will join in quickly, volunteering their own words, and they will have many of them to contribute. By having them create this list, you are simply making them *aware* of how many words they already know. In addition, you are helping them assemble a large collection of appropriate word choices that will serve them well in their subsequent writing of dialogue.

"Tom Swifties"

An old activity, but one that is still fun and pertinent and productive. It allows students to play with words and exercise their descriptive writing abilities. And it teaches them "adverbs," too.

The idea of this activity is to write single lines of dialogue in which what the person says is matched by *how* the person says it. A couple of examples will make this clear:

"Pass the *sugar*, please," she asked *sweetly*.

"Keep away from that *dog*!" he *barked*.

Notice that the words describing the way in which the persons spoke the lines seem to match the content of their remarks. Write a few examples such as these on the board and then invite students to contribute additional ones of their own. They'll surprise you with their inventions, many of which will be clever and creative. Here are some more examples to get you and your students started:

> "I think we'll have to perform by-pass surgery," said the doctor heartily.
>
> "Sure, I'd love a candy bar," she snickered.
>
> "Watch out for that crocodile!" yelled Captain Hook off-handedly.
>
> "Take the prisoner downstairs," the officer said condescendingly. [You might have to ponder this one for a moment.]
>
> "I live in Washington," she stated.

Describe a Place

After playing with words and language in some of the ways described above, students are ready to use some of this wordplay to put together some longer, more detailed descriptions. One common topic for a descriptive composition involves describing a specific place or location—a certain spot in a park; along the waterfront; a room in your house. But one must do more than simply *assign* this paper; one must also prepare students to handle the skills involved in its production. The following series of exercises can help.[2]

Read aloud to your class the following passage from John Steinbeck's story, *The Red Pony* (1966). Introduce the excerpt by telling the students that it is a description of a specific place, in this case a farmhouse and the surrounding buildings and yard. Students should listen carefully to try to visualize the location of the various items mentioned in the description:

> When they had disappeared over the crown of the ridge, Jody walked up the hill in back of the house. The dogs trotted around the house corner hunching their shoulders and grinning horribly with pleasure. Jody patted their heads—Doubletree Mutt with the big thick tail and yellow eyes, and Smasher, the shepherd, who had killed a coyote and lost an ear in doing it. Smasher's one good ear stood up higher than a collie's ear should. Billy Buck said that always happened. After the frenzied greeting the dogs lowered their noses to the ground in a businesslike way and went ahead, looking back now and then to make sure that the boy was coming. They walked up through

the chicken yard and saw the quail eating with the chickens. Smasher chased the chickens a little to keep in practice in case there should ever be sheep to herd. Jody continued on through the large vegetable patch where the green corn was higher than his head. The cow pumpkins were green and small yet. He went on to the sagebrush line where the cold spring ran out of its pipe and fell into a round wooden tub. He leaned over and drank close to the green mossy wood where the water tasted best. Then he turned and looked back on the ranch, on the low, whitewashed house girded with red geraniums, and on the long bunkhouse by the cypress tree where Billy Buck lived alone. Jody could see the great black kettle under the cypress tree. That was where the pigs were scalded. The sun was coming over the ridge now, glaring on the whitewash of the houses and barns, making the wet grass blaze softly. Behind him, in the tall sagebrush, the birds were scampering on the ground, making a great noise among the dry leaves; the squirrels piped shrilly on the side hills. Jody looked along at the far buildings. He felt an uncertainty in the air, a feeling of change and of loss and of the gain of new and unfamiliar things. Over the hillside two big black buzzards sailed low to the ground and their shadows slipped smoothly and quickly ahead of them. Some animal had died in the vicinity. Jody knew it. It might be a cow or it might be the remains of a rabbit. The buzzards overlooked nothing. Jody hated them as all decent things hate them, but they could not be hurt because they made away with carrion. (5–6)

Hand out a copy of this description and ask students to draw a picture or map of the farmyard, being sure to include all the items mentioned in the passage. You might have students work in pairs and invite students to draw their map on the board. After all the drawings are completed, ask a couple of volunteers to explain why they placed certain items where they did—"Where does it tell you in the text that the 'round wooden tub' goes there?"—for instance.

Most of the students' drawings will be similar in their placement of the various buildings and items, and this similarity should be noted. Why the similarity, and how were students able to draw the map in the first place? To find out, direct students to go through the passage one more time, circling those words and phrases that enabled them to determine where different things were located. After 2 to 3 minutes, ask for volunteers to read some of the words they circled and create a list of these words on the board. Your list, as you and your students will see, consists of *prepositions*, those words indicating *direction*. Some of the prepositions used in Steinbeck's description include "over," "up," "behind," "around," "to," and "through." Students will continue to add other prepositions to this list as they create a word bank that they can use in the following activities.

Having read Steinbeck's description of a specific place, the students are ready to try writing a description of their own. They will need to create a series of word pictures, describing objects clearly and vividly and placing them in the scene they are trying to sketch.

Prepare them for this task in the following way. Have students draw a giant "T" on their paper:

On the top line of the "T", students should identify the location they are going to describe. Have them try for something different, maybe even fantastical: Santa's workshop on Christmas Eve; a rainbow factory; a forest scene from a fairy tale. I used a *cave* for my example in class. After writing the name of their location on the top, students should list five to seven *things* that might be found in their location. This list should be made in the left-hand column of the "T":

A Cave

1. rocks
2. vines
3. bones
4. treasure
5. spider webs

Then on the right-hand side of the "T", students should compile a word bank of words and phrases that might be used to describe *each* of the items listed on the left. Such a word bank might look like this:

A Cave	
1. rocks	1. dusty; slippery; cracks
2. vines	2. tangled, twisted; moss covered; hanging from the ceiling
3. bones	3. jagged, sharp, glistening in the light; pieces; fragments

Students may spend quite a bit of time on this step of the process, but that's fine because they are collecting adjectives and phrases that will serve them well when they actually begin writing their description. Encourage students to begin their draft whenever they feel they are ready. At some point, each student will move smoothly from listing words and phrases to drafting the description itself. Be sure to emphasize to the students that they are not expected to use everything they have listed in their word bank; the material is there only as a reference. Anything there can be ignored, and other words and phrases may be added or substituted during the actual writing. But this preparatory work will have helped to focus students' attention and give them some language, images, and ideas to work with as they engage in their initial drafting. The result should be a one- or two-paragraph description of a specific place, one that appeals to the reader's senses through the use of clear, vivid language and images. For example:

The Cave
He entered the cave, a cavernous black hole yawning at him. He stepped into the darkness, brushing past a mass of tangled, twisted vines that stretched down from an invisible ceiling toward him. Suddenly, he tripped, his hands jerking out instinctively in front of him to cushion his fall. A cry of pain exploded from his lungs as his hands impaled themselves on a pile of jagged white bones scraped clean and glistening in the single shaft of pale blue light that shone dimly from a crack in the furry, moss-covered wall.

In their descriptive paragraphs, students should use words and create images that appeal to more than one of the reader's senses. The following brief exercise will focus attention on this point and can be conducted once students have completed their rough draft.

Announce to the students that, as you read aloud the following descriptive passage, students should try to guess what place is being described. As soon as they think they know the answer, they should *not* yell it out, but instead, simply raise their hand as an indication that they have figured it out:

> As she entered the darkened room, she felt the cool air against her face. Trying to make as little noise as possible, she made her way down the aisle. The smell of buttered popcorn became stronger as she struggled into her seat.

Not many students will raise their hand after the first sentence. Only a couple of clues are given—descriptions that appeal to the listener's senses of sight ("darkened room") and touch ("cool air"). But the location remains vague: it could be a closet, an attic . . . almost anything. The second sentence helps to narrow down the choices considerably. The clue that appeals to the listener's sense of hearing ("Trying to make as little noise as possible . . .") and the mention of "the aisle" leads the listener to think of a church or perhaps a school assembly or a theater. More student hands will be raised, then, at the end of this sentence. The third sentence clinches it with its description of "The smell of buttered popcorn" and the situation of the character struggling to get into her seat: it's a movie theater. It's quite a sight to see all the students raise their hands immediately and simultaneously as this third sentence is read.

Students see the point that the passage has utilized images appealing to the various senses as a way to reveal the location being described. Invite students to create a similar paragraph of their own: select a specific location and reveal its identity through a multisensory description. For example:

> The doors opened and he stepped forward into a crowd of people, pushing and shoving to find room to stand. The whirring of the motor signaled the start of the dropping motion that always tickled his stomach and made him clench his teeth against the feeling.

Read some of the students' descriptions aloud to the class, asking them once again to raise their hands when they think they have figured out the location. This exercise should make students more aware of the importance of a multisensory approach to their descriptions. After completing this activity, instruct students to return to their *original* descriptions of places and revise them by adding phrases and images that appeal to different senses.

"Describe . . ."

Having played with words and images and learned to appeal to the various senses, students are ready to engage in more formal, detailed descriptive compositions. The NCTE publication *What Can I Write About? 7000 Topics for High School Students,* by David Powell (1981), lists several good possibilities for papers, including the following subjects:

> Describe . . .
>
> a morning rain
>
> an approaching storm
>
> sand castles
>
> the view from a hilltop overlooking a great city
>
> a fox seeing a movement in the grass
>
> the flight of an eagle
>
> a ghost town
>
> a condemned hotel (2–3, 8)

Additionally, you and your students can create your own topics for writing. Here are some more ideas for starters:

> Describe . . .
>
> a giant striding across the land
>
> a tree in the wind
>
> a flower that is opening
>
> a person selling shoes
>
> bacon cooking in a pan
>
> a child learning to walk
>
> the sun coming up in the morning
>
> a child who desperately wants to be picked for a team
>
> an old person gathering wood in the snow and building a fire
>
> a mechanical toy
>
> the worst meal you've ever eaten
>
> a pinball machine in action
>
> a parent scolding a child

Following are some examples written to these starters:

> "Describe . . . a giant striding across the land."
>
> The villagers first became aware of Gordo's approach when they noticed the swaying leaves on the trees and the restless,

jerky movements of the animals. Then the distant thunder started: a low, deep rumble rising to a series of booming, bone-shuddering thuds. Looking up suddenly, fearfully, the villagers shivered as Gordo's shadow fell across them, sweeping black night onto their fields and the mountains beyond. Then the footsteps came. First, the village lake disappeared in a splashing, drenching wall of water. Whole fields lay drowned in the overflow. Then the craters appeared wherever Gordo trudged: vast, yawning chasms with sheer cliffs dropping hundreds of feet to a packed-mud floor below. Gordo had come!

"Describe . . . the worst meal you've ever eaten"

I knew I was in trouble when I had to kill 13 flies in order to clean off the counter stool before I could sit down. My hand slid along the counter-top, propelled on a bed of grease, as I reached for the egg-spattered menu. Prying apart the two pages stuck together by a week-old glop of syrup, I spied an item that I thought might, once gobbled down, *stay* down.

"I'd like coffee, eggs, and toast, please," I spoke to the server, a gum-cracking, pimply-faced youth whose body seemed to be in a dilemma about whether to grow up or give up.

"Hey, Sam!" she bellowed, evidently talking to the cook in back, "Two eggs and stuff!"

"Got it!" yelled Sam.

The coffee came first, a steaming mug of muddy darkness whose surface roiled with blast-furnace heat. Surely the Armed Forces had used this vile chemical creation as a defoliant in a war somewhere years earlier, and here is how they have recycled the surplus.

The server appeared again, shoving a large plate toward me that clanked harshly on the cracked Formica counter. On this plate lay two alien, waxy-yellow moon-rocks, four jagged burnt things that had been toast 85 degrees earlier, and a sprawling tangle of stringy potatoes that were freshly oiled and lubed.

My breakfast had arrived.

Notes

1. Part of the "Synesthesia" exercise is based on an activity in Dodd (1973, 12).

2. The first activity in this "Describe a Place" exercise (using the passage from Steinbeck's *The Red Pony*) was inspired by a conference presentation made by Julia Gottesman, formerly the language arts supervisor in the Los Angeles, California Public Schools.

Works Cited

Dodd, Anne Wescott. 1973. *Write Now! Insights into Creative Writing.* New York: Globe.

Powell, David. 1981. *What Can I Write About? 7000 Topics for High School Students.* Urbana: National Council of Teachers of English.

Schulz, Charles M. 1962. *Happiness Is a Warm Puppy.* London: Paul Hamlyn, Ltd.

Steinbeck, John. 1966. *The Red Pony.* New York: Bantam.

6 Developing Voice and Tone

Voices from Beyond the Grave

When I first tried to develop students' sense of "voice" and "tone" in their writing, I used a composition topic that I thought would provide a terrific stimulus for a strong, emotional narrative: "Write about the most terrifying (or sad or lonely or ???) experience you have ever had." Perfect! How can you avoid having a distinct voice or tone come through in your writing when describing such an emotional incident? Well, it didn't work. I got such stuff as "I had climbed this tree in the backyard one day and I fell and broke my arm and it hurt SOOOO bad." Almost every account sounded as if the author were reporting the six o'clock news: bland, monotone, dull, lifeless. It was just after I had received the students' disappointing drafts, in fact, that I saw an article in an issue of Scholastic's *Scope* magazine that described an activity aimed at exactly this skill. So I tried the activity just to see what would happen—and I have been using it ever since. Better fasten your seat belt for this one—it's powerful stuff. All the examples here were written in class by students of mine during the past few years.

The activity is called "Voices from Beyond the Grave,"[1] and the directions are as follows:

> Become someone else, someone old or young or sad or ???
> Imagine that you have died, and now you are looking back and
> commenting on an aspect of your past life. What will you say?

Following are some compelling responses from my students:

> I was 12 years old and I guess I was a bad girl 'cause
> Momma hurt me a lot. But I know it was my fault since I never
> did what I was told or finished my chores. So, late one night, I
> decided to hurt myself, too. I took this knife and, well . . . you
> know.
> I thought Momma kinda liked me, but I guess not . . .
>
> —Diana

> I suppose one day I'd have been famous. But I got involved
> with the alcoholics. Then when I was hittin' the bottle, men
> broke into my house. They took everything—my china, my
> crystal—even my life!
>
> —Penny

I was a flop in high school. I could never do anything right. I thought my grades were awful, and *I* was awful, too. I didn't have any friends. I never made it to 12th grade. I dropped out, and I don't mean just from school!

—Susan

I was only a year old. My mommy told me to stay out of the street, but I didn't listen. So when Mommy wasn't looking, I went out there to play. I guess Mommy was right.

—Raichell

These are powerful pieces of writing. The best ones have a "Bang!" at the end, and the students work hard to move their words and phrasing around so as to attain that effect.

But not all the voices have to be serious and "heavy" in tone. Sometimes they can actually be humorous:

I was 32 and an excellent motorcycle rider. I could take corners, jump and go fast. I could do *anything* but go through trees.

—Mike

The lumberjack yelled, "Watch out for that falling tree!!" Like an idiot, I just stood there and said, "Where?"

—Melissa

I was a gunslinger. "The Best in the West," some people said. Too bad I wasn't as good as the "Best in the East."

—Chris

This activity invites students to play with language, use puns, and put phrases together in unusual ways to show contrasts and other special effects:

When I was 10, Mom told me to look both ways for cars. But she never said anything about "trucks."

—Lisa

I was a famous magician who could do some great tricks. One of them went too far. Now you see me, now you don't.

—Shannon

I loved flying kites. Once my kite strayed into the telephone wires. Boy! Was I shocked!

—Ryan

> I was going to a party that night. My dad said, "If you get
> drunk tonight, don't even THINK about coming back!" Well, I
> did, so I didn't.
>
> —Jason

Other voices achieve quite an impact by understating the situation.
Though little information is given, it is still sufficient:

> Forty people die every day from drunk-driving. Last Thursday
> it was forty-one.
>
> —Wendy

> Walking is supposed to be good for your health. But crossing
> the street against the light isn't.
>
> —Angela

> Have you ever heard the expression, "Lightning never strikes
> twice"? Don't believe it!
>
> —Heather

Finally, there are some other ones that . . . umm . . . produce a whole
different effect:

> "Keep your eyes on the road," they say. After I hit the car, they
> <u>were</u>.
>
> —Eric

> I was against the seat-belt law. Now I'm against the dashboard.
>
> —Ben

Students don't need a lecture about "voice" and "tone." A couple of
models of "Voices from Beyond the Grave" and they get the point.
They *hear* the voice and *feel* the effect. As they draft these pieces, they
work together to get their writing focused, tight, and powerful. They
don't need the teacher, either, to tell them when their "voice" has
"arrived." They know. And when it works out well—as many of their
pieces do—it is powerful, indeed:

> I was very sick and Mommy said I might die. I wished upon a
> star that I would get better because Mommy also told me that
> wishes sometimes come true. Sometimes.
>
> —Alexi

This exercise, by the way, might be used as an excellent introduction
to a reading of *Spoon River Anthology* by Edgar Lee Masters. This
literature, after all, is a series of *extended* voices from beyond the grave,
and students' work with their *own* "voices" will provide them with an

understanding and preparation that will serve them well when they read Masters's writing.

Monologues and Dialogues

The elements of voice and tone become most apparent when one is talking *to* an audience. A perfect example to illustrate this point is the difference in tone that a caller adopts when he or she is speaking into your automatic answering machine at home. You play back the tape to hear who has called while you were away, and you hear these voices—all monotone in quality—delivering a message or making a request. The reason for the monotone voice is that it is difficult for the callers to *imagine* or pretend that the audience is there when they know that, in reality, they are talking to a machine (and how excited can you get when talking to an object?). So writing assignments that make the audience close and visible have a better chance of bringing out a strong, distinct tone from the writer.

Such assignments may be found in the writing of monologues and dialogues. These kinds of writing, as well as many other valuable activities, are included in the *Active Voices* books (Moffett 1987), a valuable resource.

I direct students to write drafts of the four assignments below, one after another. After completing each draft, the students share them in small groups, selecting one of the papers to be read aloud to the entire class. Then we simply move on to the next assignment and repeat the sharing process. After all four drafts are completed, the students select *one* of their papers to revise, edit, and polish. They will spend as long as a week working on their revisions. During this time they will move back and forth between revising individually and working in small groups to offer and obtain feedback.

Having students make a final copy of only *one* of their papers has a couple of advantages: first, while not every one of the students' four drafting efforts will result in an excellent paper, it is likely that at least *one* of them will, and this is the one that students should revise and hand in as representative of their best work during this unit. Second, by having students polish only one of their papers, you are able to control the paper load for yourself. Imagine having to read, review, and grade all four papers from each student.

Following are examples of each of the four assignments: (1) a *dialogue* written in play form; (2) an *exterior monologue* (one person—who does all the talking—speaks to another); (3) an *interior monologue* (in which we hear the character's inner voice as he or she experiences a situation—the character is "talking" to himself or herself); and (4) *communication through correspondence* (an exchange between two or more persons accomplished entirely through written correspondence—letters, notes, etc.).

Dialogue in Play Form

Pilot: This is Cloud Lines flight #473 requesting clearance to land.

Tower: This is Seattle tower. Maintain altitude for 8 minutes, then turn for a northern approach. . . . is that you, John?

Pilot: Marsha?? What are you doing in the tower? I thought you had stopped working on air traffic. And when can I come in? My flight's late already.

Tower: Just cool your jets, John. I had to go back to work to support myself after you flew off in the night with that flight attendant. By the way, you two still playing with each other's seat belts?

Pilot: Still the same old Marsha, aren't you? Just get me in now, and we can talk about this later.

Tower: You can stay up there till the runway freezes over, for all I care! I've still got about 3 planes ahead of you, so check back with me next Thursday.

Pilot: Marsha! I'm late already! You can't do this to me. Help me out!

Tower: Oh, all right. Turn 34 degrees right and proceed east 10 miles.

Pilot (relieved): Okay, thanks . . . (pause) . . . Marsha!! That'll send me right into the side of Mt. Rainier.

Tower: I know. Hahahaha. Just kidding! Okay, come in on the north runway, but don't start lowering your flaps at me when you arrive. I'm taking off myself. It's been a long day. And you just made it a lot longer.

Exterior Monologue

"Hospital Admissions—may I help you? . . . Well, fine, of course we'll get your husband up to a room, but first . . . yes, I know he's bleeding! I can see the blood on the floor there . . . Orderly! Will you clean up this mess, please? Thank you.

"Uh . . . would you be so kind as to move your husband over to the left a little so we can clean up here? . . . Well, just roll him over, or take hold of his ankles and drag him, for all I care. Just get him off the carpet! Is he like this at home? Ma'am, you have my sympathy.

"Now, about these forms you need to fill out: here's the Insurance form and the Patient's Doctor form and the Blood Type form. . . . No, we can't put it off till later; we have rules here, y'know.

"Now, fill out these forms and then we'll just pack Mr. Messy there off to the 4th floor. . . . What? He died?? You sure?? Well, in that case, I have this Next-of-Kin form you need to fill out. It's normal procedure—'par for the corpse,' you might say, ha, ha, ha! . . . Well, the same to you, too, Lady!"

Interior Monologue

I'm going to fail. I know it! I don't know this stuff. Ralph was right: I should've read those chapters. Well, maybe I can fake it. Just use big words; say a lot of "I think . . ." and "Perhaps it might be true that . . ." Yeah, that'll do it! Teacher will think I'm brilliant because it'll look like I'm considering all the possibilities.

But what's this test all about, anyway? Darn! I wish I'd read those chapters. I didn't even look at the titles! They could be about the social behavior of kangaroos, for all I know.

Okay, here's the test. Let's see the bad news:

"DISCUSS THE CAUSES OF THE CIVIL WAR."

What war was this? A "civil" war? No war is civil. It's always brutal and UN-civilized. Maybe it was a civil war because it wasn't really a war at all. That's it! That's what I'll say. Let's see now. . . .

"EVERYONE HAS DISAGREEMENTS AT SOME POINT IN TIME. . . ."

Yeah, that sounds good. ". . . some point in time." She'll like that. Sounds serious.

"IN THIS SO-CALLED 'CIVIL WAR', THEN, SOME PEOPLE . . ."

Wish I knew where this war took place: China? Russia? Hawaii? Can't keep saying "These people" all the time. She'll get suspicious. Okay, what've I got so far?

"IN THIS SO-CALLED 'CIVIL WAR,' THEN, SOME PEOPLE . . . HAD A DISAGREEMENT . . ."

About what? I don't know. Taxes? Government? Could be about the price of parking meters, for all I know.

". . . ABOUT A SUBJECT SO IMPORTANT, SO CENTRAL TO THEIR WELL-BEING AND WAY OF LIFE THAT . . ."

Yeah, teacher will love this stuff. Oh, you ARE a smooth one. You oughta bottle your brains and sell them. You could retire early and live like a millionaire.

"... THAT THEY WERE WILLING TO GO TO WAR OVER IT. BUT THEN, BECAUSE THEY WERE A CLEVER PEOPLE ..."

Whoever these people were; with my luck, they were really anteaters, and this was a war over control of the biggest anthill in the forest.

"... BECAUSE THEY WERE A CLEVER PEOPLE, THEY RE-SOLVED THEIR DIFFERENCES IN A UNIQUE FASHION ..."

Oh, this is so slick, you could put it at the top of a ski slope and it would win the prize for the longest slide.

"... AND SHOWED THAT PERHAPS IT MIGHT BE TRUE THAT WARS CAN INDEED BE CIVIL INSTEAD OF BRUTAL."

Hot Dog! That's fantastic! Hey, Teach! Just give me my "A" now and you can use my paper for an Answer Key. I can't wait to see what the teacher thinks of THIS one. Wow! Is SHE in for a surprise!

Communication through Correspondence

To Whom It May Concern:

I am returning the record album you sent me, *Top Ten Bird Calls of the Pacific Northwest,* because I do not want it, and I didn't order it, either. You sent it to me because it is your "Album-of-the-Month" selection, but I am returning it to you within the proper time limit specified on my membership agreement. So please credit my account.

Thank you,

Harvey Hornswallow

Dear Preferred Customer,

We think of you as our special, preferred customer because of your willingness to pay promptly for the albums you purchase from us. Recently, however, we noticed that you have not yet paid for the latest album we sent you, a treasured recording of the *Top Ten Bird Calls of the Pacific Northwest.* You showed such good taste in selecting this album for your record library. Surely it will become a priceless item that you will want to play again and again for years to come. Won't you show your good taste also in returning the purchase price to us immediately? We want to keep your good name on our special list of preferred customers.

Thank you,

P. J. Peckinpoop

Dear Mr. Peckinpoop,

By now you should have received my letter telling you that I was returning your *Bird Calls.* I don't want it, I didn't order it, and I'm not paying for it. Hope this takes care of the matter.

Thank you,

Harvey Hornswallow

Dear Customer,

Our records show that you still owe us for an album we sent you last month, a stirring, lovely series entitled *Top Ten Bird Calls of the Pacific Northwest.* Surely you have played this treasure a hundred times by now. And we don't blame you for your enthusiasm. But if it is as important to you as it is to our other valued customers to keep your good name on our special list, then please send in payment immediately.

Thank you,

P. J. Peckinpoop

Dear Mr. Poop,

This is the third letter I've written to tell you that I don't want your stupid album of stupid bird calls. I don't like birds. I spend my evenings shooting birds out of trees and picking them off the telephone wires. Every Sunday I poison pigeons in the park. I hate birds! So why in the world would I want to keep your Bird Calls album for anything other than target practice? Do you understand now? I don't have your album and I want you to credit my account immediately.

Hornswallow

Dear Harve,

Frankly, I am puzzled. You say that you do not like our feathered friends, and yet you have ordered one of our most popular records of the *Top Ten Bird Calls of the Pacific Northwest.* How can this be? Surely you are, like me, a true fan of our flying, furry creatures.

Won't you take care of this matter of your long-overdue bill soon? Your friends here in the office will thank you for your cooperation.

P. J.

Dear Poop,

I am resigning from your record club. I do not want any more of your records. I do not want any more of you and your stupid letters. Take my name off your Preferred Customer list and destroy it. Forget that I have ever lived.

Don't try to write back, either. I'm moving—tomorrow—to another state far, far away from here. In fact, I've already moved. Ha, ha, ha! You'll never catch me now.

Hornswallow

Dear Preferred Customer,

Because you ordered our best-selling album last month, *Top Ten Bird Calls of the Pacific Northwest,* we have taken the liberty of sending to you a companion volume, a delightful, two-record set of *Mating Calls of the Yellow-Headed Sapsuckers and Other Romantic Birds.* This is one set I know you'll want to have. If you wish to keep the records, do nothing. We will bill you automatically. Thank you for being one of our favorite customers. We look forward to hearing from you often.

Sincerely,

P. J. Peckinpoop

Writing for an Audience

An important skill in writing is the ability to maintain a focus on one's audience, anticipating the audience's need for clarification or explanation at various points in one's narrative. The following assignment helps develop this sense of audience-awareness.

Mr. Rogers

This assignment involves explaining a concept or an idea to a young child. For an excellent example of this activity, students need only to watch one episode of "Mr. Rogers' Neighborhood,"[2] the popular children's TV show that appears daily. Fred Rogers demonstrates an outstanding ability to zero in on his audience: his choice of topics, his use of language and examples are all aimed directly and appropriately at his audience of young children. Some years ago, Rogers published a children's book in which he discusses some pertinent subjects of interest and concern to his young audience. His subjects included these items:

Getting Shots	Learning about Hot Things
Swimming	Being Careful about Cars
Playing Safely	Taking Care of Your Teeth
Watching TV	Taking Care of Yourself

Here is an example, taken from his book, showing how Rogers explains one of these concepts:

Getting Shots

Did you ever have a doctor or a nurse give you a shot? Well, I guess you know it's something that helps you keep from getting sick. It usually hurts a little at first—feels like a pinch—but not for long. Sometimes it doesn't hurt at all.

Of course, there's nothing wrong with crying if a shot does hurt, and it's really fine if you can talk about it. If you want to sit in someone's lap or hold someone's hand, that's not being a baby—that's helping you feel better.

Doctors and nurses don't want to hurt you; they just want to give you what they can to keep you well. [n.p.]

Notice how Rogers explains this process of getting shots. He seems to have an intuitive sense of just how much information to include, even using a comparison ("feels like a pinch") to make his point more understandable to his young audience. A little reassurance at the end, and he has put together a clear, pleasant, appropriate presentation that appeals directly to children.

I read Rogers's example above to my students and show them the list of other topics covered in his book. Then, I give the directions for the writing assignment:

"It is *your* turn now. Explain a concept or an idea to a young child. You may use one of Rogers's topics or choose one of your own. But make your explanation clear for your audience through your use of appropriate language and phrasing. Obtain responses to your rough draft and suggestions for revision from your classmates."

Here's one of my own examples:

Helping Around the House

It's nice to have Mom and Dad make your dinner for you, isn't it? Your parents do a lot of other nice things, too: they make sure that you have clean clothes every day, they vacuum the carpet to keep it clean, and they sweep and dust all around your house. All these things are a lot of work, so I'm sure that your parents would appreciate your help. See if you can help them, for instance, by keeping your own room clean. Pick up your clothes and put your toys away when you are finished playing with them. Your parents will be happy to see that you can take care of your own things. You might also help your parents wash and dry the dishes after dinner. This is an important job that will be done faster and will be more fun if you help with it.

What other ways can you think of to help around the house?

This assignment is not an easy one to complete. Students need help in zeroing in on this particular audience: sometimes they talk about inappropriate subjects or provide too much detail; other times they need to change their choice of words or to define their terms. One student, for instance, writing about watching TV, said: "Watching TV can be lots of fun. . . . but watching too much TV can make you, well, turn into a blob." Another student, probably trying to be helpful in his description of the dangers of taking poisons, went a little bit too far: "If you took those, you could drop dead in a matter of minutes. It would be a very painful death too. Like needles going down your throat. Now that isn't very pleasant, is it boys and girls?"

Sometimes students say something that they didn't mean to say. In this example, the writer unintentionally equates dentists with "monsters":

> The monsters will also cause owies in your mouth and then you would have to go to a dentist. Dentists are people that drill and pull bad teeth caused by cavities. So if you brush your teeth after every meal, you can keep the monsters and the dentists from hurting you.

Finally, a problem occurs when the writer momentarily drops his or her sense of audience entirely, as in this example:

> When you come in with a cavity, the dentist will put you in his chair and tell you to open your mouth. He will then numb the tooth with novocaine. Novocaine makes the tooth so you can't feel it. Then he will stick a small drill in your mouth. To try and make you feel better he'll tell you not to worry and that it won't hurt. But it always does. . . .

The last sentence suddenly takes on the tone of "Can we talk? Can we be honest here for a moment?" Students need to be made aware of such changes in their stance toward their audience.

With revision, students' writing on this assignment becomes focused, clear, and concise. The final effort reveals students' ability to maintain their focus on a specific audience and adapt their language and writing style appropriately. Often the final copy is quite good, and sometimes it is outstanding, as in the following student example:

When Parents Are Divorced

> Do you live with both of your parents? Some of your friends might not. Mothers and fathers who live in different houses have decided not to be married anymore. This is called a divorce.
>
> Parents get divorced because they cannot get along anymore. When our parents get a divorce, some of us think it might be our fault. This is not true. You did not do anything wrong.

Some parents get married to a new person after a divorce. This means that you will have a new mother or father, and maybe even some new brothers and sisters. This is very special. Not everyone has two families to take care of them.

A divorce is not a good thing, and it is okay to feel sad if it happens. If you feel strange or bad or even scared, talking about the divorce with your parents or someone you trust will always help. I want you to remember that your mother and father will always love you very much, and nothing, not even a divorce, will change that.

—Kim-An

I have used the "Mr. Rogers" exercise successfully with both junior high/middle school and senior high school students, but if you are teaching at the senior high level, you might want a different topic designed specifically for older, more mature students. The following assignment is most appropriate for high school juniors and seniors, but it develops the same skill of audience awareness as does the "Mr. Rogers" essay.

"Tell Us about Yourself"

Almost every application form for either college or a job has a section that asks the applicant to "Tell us about yourself." Sometimes the section is phrased as a request for information about the applicant's interests or academic record; other times it asks for an opinion about why the applicant wishes to apply for this particular position or to attend this specific university. The following excerpt from the University of California's Undergraduate Application Packet (1987–1988 version) is a typical example of what a student is likely to encounter:

Section VIII: Essay—All Applicants

The essay is an important part of your application. It will help admissions officers gain a more complete picture of you. Use the essay to tell about yourself. Any of the following topics are appropriate to discuss: your goals and aspirations, what is important to you and the reasons why; your academic interests; school and community activities and achievements; work experiences; or educational and career objectives . . . .

Five hundred words is a good length for the essay. The essay should be legible.

This section of a college or job application form, although worded in any of several different ways, almost always includes a request to "Tell us about yourself." This, then, becomes an appropriate and worthwhile writing assignment for students in class. It provides them with a rehearsal of responses that they might make to a real request for such information. In my precollege writing classes, composed mainly of seniors, I had the students work on this assignment fairly early in the school year so that they could use their final copy (or parts of it) when filling out applications to universities in the spring. The relevance of this assignment—and the specific audience involved for the writing—are readily understood by the students. The quality of the final copies usually reflects this understanding and resultant commitment to the task.

Notes

1. I want to express my appreciation to Richard Robinson, president of Scholastic, Inc., and to Margaret Stevaralgia, Scholastic's reference librarian, for allowing me to use this exercise, even when our combined searches could not turn up the original source from many years ago.

2. I want to express my sincere thanks to Fred Rogers not only for giving me permission to use the excerpt in my book, but also for taking the time to write to me personally in response to my request.

Works Cited

Moffett, James. 1987. *Active Voices.* Books I, II, and III. Upper Montclair, NJ: Boynton/Cook.

Rogers, Fred. n.d. "Mister Rogers Talks to Kids." Pittsburgh: Family Communications, Inc./Blue Cross, Blue Shield of Western Pennsylvania.

7 Narrative Writing Activities

Narrative writing serves an "informing" function, reporting events that happened or telling stories. Two skills involved in this kind of communication are the placement of events in an appropriate sequence and the selection of details to include in the story. The "Personal Experience" paper, for example, is a valuable exercise for developing these skills. The following activities are some others that I have used with my students:

Telling a Story One-Word-at-a-Time

The series of activities below serves to focus students' attention on the skills involved in narrative speaking and writing. It can also be used as an introduction to the presentation and discussion of the essential elements of a story.

Step 1. "Today in class we are all going to participate in the telling of a story. Now, I want to be fair about this and make sure that each person has an equal chance to contribute, so let's tell the story *one word at a time.* I'll start with the first word, and then Raymond, you add a word, and then we'll continue up and down the rows until everyone has had a chance to contribute. Feel free to start a new sentence whenever it seems appropriate, and don't take a long time to think of what to say next; just listen carefully to how the story is developing and then add on your word quickly."

This activity not only leads students to focus on the idea of "sequence"—it also develops their listening abilities. Students are careful to listen to the words contributed by their classmates, knowing that their turn will come to add on a word that will "fit," that will build on the words and events that have already occurred and so keep the story moving along. This will be difficult to do if one has not been listening closely to what students have said before and how the story is developing through the various one-word contributions. If, for some reason, the story seems to be going nowhere, simply stop and then start a new story with the next student in line volunteering the first word.

Step 2. It won't take students long to catch on to the way the above exercise proceeds and to be able to contribute their word quickly to the building story. The problem is that the students don't have the opportunity to participate *often*. With 25 to 30 students in the class, it takes quite a while for the story to come around for students to make a *second* word contribution. So, follow up this initial activity by having students break into small groups of five or six students each. Now, each group should try the same exercise, one student in each group volunteering the first word and the others adding on to it. With this structure, students will be participating frequently, contributing every fifth or sixth word to the story. Instruct the groups that, if they should find that their story, for whatever reason, doesn't seem to be working out and building appropriately, they should simply start a new story with a new beginning word.

Step 3. "We're going to try this exercise again as a whole class, but this time we're going to tell a story one *sentence* at a time." Sometimes I will add a suggestion that we should try to tell a science fiction story. So my first sentence might be: "The rocket was set for blast-off." Then, Vincent will contribute the second sentence, and so on up and down the rows until the whole class has had a chance to contribute to the story. I have also had the class build a mystery ("There were three loud knocks at the door, and then silence") and a fairy tale. Do this variation first as a whole class, and then break students into small groups again so they can add on a sentence more frequently.

Step 4. Having practiced building a story cooperatively—first by adding one word, and then one sentence, at a time—students are ready to try making extended contributions to a group effort. They should assemble in small groups consisting of five students each. Instruct each student in the group to begin writing a story *individually*, but add these directions: "Write only a description of the *setting* of this story—where and when does it take place? Set the scene with as vivid and detailed a description as you can." Allow 5 to 6 minutes for the writing. At the end of this time, ask the students to stop and pass their paper to the person sitting on their left. Each student now has another group member's story in front of them. They should read what has been written so far and then add on to it, but with these instructions: "Introduce the main characters. Who are they? What do they do? What do they look like? What else do you know about them? Anything you can tell us about these characters will be helpful."

After 7 to 10 more minutes of writing, have the students stop and pass their paper to the left once more. They should once again read what has been written so far and then add on to the story by describing the *problem* that the characters must solve. The next time that the papers are passed to the left, students will add on to the new story in front of them by *complicating* the problem: "No matter what the problem is that the characters are facing—no matter how bad the situation is—*make it worse.*" After students write for several minutes on this aspect of the story, the papers are passed to the left for the last time, and the students are directed to *resolve* the story, to write the ending: "What happens? How does it all work out?" Allow time at the end of this exercise for students to read the various stories that were produced cooperatively in their group.

Step 5. An appropriate follow-up to the above sequence of activities involves students in completing unfinished stories. Look in publishers' catalogues for books of unfinished stories that students might use for this purpose. Or read aloud the beginning of a short story and have students write an appropriate ending. Students are learning about the concept of "coherence," coming to realize that the ending must take into account and flow naturally from what has occurred previously in the story.

A variation of this follow-up activity is to have students write their own beginning for an unfinished story, stopping at a suspenseful point. I point out that suspense is a feeling of wanting to know "What will happen next?" So one can arouse this feeling in the reader by creating problems for the characters to work through but not resolving them immediately. Complicate the situation—make it worse—without writing the ending that ends the reader's suspense about what will happen next.

Writing a Character Sketch

A good character sketch involves *showing*, not telling, what a person or character is like. This is "telling":

> Wendy was angry when she came into class this morning. I mean, she was really, really, REALLY angry!!

This is "showing":

> Wendy flung open the door to the classroom, stomped to her desk in the back of the room, threw herself into her seat, and slammed her books to the floor.
> "What's wrong, Wendy?" her friend asked.
> "Shut up!" Wendy snarled.

"Showing" involves a description of what the character says and does that reveals the character's mood and personality. It makes a character sketch come alive and allows the reader to come to know the person through that person's words and actions. Helping students see the distinction between "showing" and "telling," then, is a good way to prepare them for writing a character sketch.

To allow students to practice this approach of *showing* rather than *telling*, I hand out a sheet listing several emotions and feelings and moods accompanied by the following instructions and suggestions[1]:

Here is a list of words that describes the ways that people feel at times:

angry	depressed	disappointed
enthusiastic	fearful	frenzied
grouchy	happy	immature
joyous	miserable	moody
proud	reckless	revengeful
sad	shy	silly
tormented	troubled	vicious
violent	wild	arrogant
defeated	compassionate	thoughtful
excited	lonely	afraid

Directions: Create a scene in which a character displays one of these emotions. Following are questions to consider:

Who will your character be?

What will he or she be doing?

Where is your character? At home? At school? Alone? Or with others?

What has happened to him or her? Why does your character feel this way?

Suggestions:

Make your character believable and realistic.

Describe things in detail so your audience can "see" the action.

Use dialogue to help move the story along.

Some examples:

Impatient

Her math class sixth period seemed to last a thousand years. She stared intently at the clock on the wall, wishing that, somehow, she could push the hands around the clock simply with her eyes. The seconds ticked by slowly, the second hand moving past the 2, now the 3, crawling toward 4 and 5. Ten minutes more—each minute lasting an hour—and she would be free. She had it all planned with the precision of a space shuttle launch: out the door, turn right, three doors down to the next hallway, turn left, grab the phone (she clutched the quarter in her pocket, rubbing it hard between her fingers). Dial the number of the hospital and—at last! find out the results of her mother's surgery.

Nervous

He sat there stiffly in his seat in the classroom, flipping the pages of his textbook, trying to photograph every formula on every page, going over each explanation. He shot a glance at the clock: two minutes till the bell. Then he'd face it at last—the final exam that would determine whether he passed the course, or failed. He remembered the teacher's words last week: "I don't know, Dave. It doesn't look good. You've missed six assignments and turned in poor tests every time."

"I can do it, Mr. Anders. I really can. I KNOW this stuff."

"Well," Mr. Anders replied, "We'll see. The final's next week. If you receive a satisfactory score, I'll pass you. Fair enough?"

Dave was suddenly startled out of his remembrance by the ringing of the bell. He stared dumbly at Mr. Anders striding into the room, paper in hand. He slowly closed his book and placed it carefully on the floor beside him, taking a copy of the exam from the teacher's extended hand.

He sighed, picked up his pencil, bent down over his desk, and started.

Once students have completed this exercise in "showing, not telling," they are ready to choose a real person as the focus for their character sketch. The success of their sketch will depend on their ability to "show" the person's character through anecdotes and actions. I introduce the assignment by reading aloud James Thurber's essay, "Snapshot of a Dog" (1945). It's a clever, descriptive, poignant story in which Thurber reveals his pet's character by telling a series of anecdotes, each story illustrating a different trait:

Snapshot of a Dog*

I ran across a dim photograph of him the other day, going through some old things. He's been dead twenty-five years. His

---

name was Rex (my two brothers and I named him when we were in our early teens) and he was a bull terrier. "An American bull terrier," we used to say, proudly; none of your English bulls. He had one brindle eye that sometimes made him look like a clown and sometimes reminded you of a politician with derby hat and cigar. The rest of him was white except for a brindle saddle that always seemed to be slipping off and a brindle stocking on a hind leg. Nevertheless, there was a nobility about him. He was big and muscular and beautifully made. He never lost his dignity even when trying to accomplish the extravagant tasks my brothers and myself used to set for him. One of these was the bringing of a ten-foot wooden rail into the yard through the back gate. We would throw it out into the alley and tell him to go get it. Rex was as powerful as a wrestler, and there were not many things that he couldn't manage somehow to get hold of with his great jaws and lift or drag to wherever he wanted to put them, or wherever we wanted them put. He could catch the rail at the balance and lift it clear of the ground and trot with great confidence toward the gate. Of course, since the gate was only four feet wide or so, he couldn't bring the rail in broadside. He found that out when he got a few terrific jolts, but he wouldn't give up. He finally figured out how to do it, by dragging the rail, holding onto one end, growling. He got a great, wagging satisfaction out of his work. We used to bet kids who had never seen Rex in action that he could catch a baseball thrown as high as they could throw it. He almost never let us down. Rex could hold a baseball with ease in his mouth, in one cheek, as if it were a chew of tobacco.

He was a tremendous fighter, but he never started fights. I don't believe he liked to get into them, despite the fact that he came from a line of fighters. He never went for another dog's throat but for one of its ears (that teaches a dog a lesson), and he would get his grip, close his eyes, and hold on. He could hold on for hours. His longest fight lasted from dusk until almost pitch-dark, one Sunday. It was fought in East Main Street in Columbus with a large, snarly nondescript that belonged to a big colored man. When Rex finally got his ear grip, the brief whirlwind of snarling turned to screeching. It was frightening to listen to and to watch. The Negro boldly picked the dogs up somehow and began swinging them around his head, and finally let them fly like a hammer in a hammer throw, but although they landed ten feet away with a great plump, Rex still held on.

The two dogs eventually worked their way to the middle of the car tracks, and after a while two or three streetcars were held up by the fight. A motorman tried to pry Rex's jaws open with a switch rod; somebody lighted a fire and made a torch of a stick and held that to Rex's tail, but he paid no attention. In the end, all the residents and storekeepers in the neighborhood were on hand, shouting this, suggesting that. Rex's joy of battle, when battle was joined, was almost tranquil. He had a kind of pleasant expression during fights, not a vicious one, his eyes closed in what would have seemed to be sleep had it not been for the turmoil of the struggle. The Oak Street Fire Department finally had to be sent for—I don't know why nobody thought of it sooner. Five or six pieces of apparatus arrived, followed by a battalion chief. A hose was attached and a powerful stream of water was turned on the dogs. Rex held on for several moments more while the torrent buffeted him about like a log in a freshet. He was a hundred yards away from where the fight started when he finally let go.

The story of that Homeric fight got all around town, and some of our relatives looked upon the incident as a blot on the family name. They insisted that we get rid of Rex, but we were very happy with him, and nobody could have made us give him up. We would have left town with him first, along any road there was to go. It would have been different, perhaps, if he'd ever started fights, or looked for trouble. But he had a gentle disposition. He never bit a person in the ten strenuous years that he lived, nor ever growled at anyone except prowlers. He killed cats, that is true, but quickly and neatly and without especial malice, the way men kill certain animals. It was the only thing he did that we could never cure him of doing. He never killed, or even chased, a squirrel. I don't know why. He had his own philosophy about such things. He never ran barking after wagons or automobiles. He didn't seem to see the idea of pursuing something you couldn't catch, or something you couldn't do anything with, even if you did catch it. A wagon was one of the things he couldn't tug along with his mighty jaws, and he knew it. Wagons, therefore, were not a part of his world.

Swimming was his favorite recreation. The first time he ever saw a body of water (Alum Creek), he trotted nervously along the steep bank for a while, fell to barking wildly, and finally plunged in from a height of eight feet or more. I shall always remember that shining, virgin dive. Then he swam upstream and back just for the pleasure of it, like a man. It was fun to see him battle upstream against a stiff current, struggling and growling every foot of the way. He had as much fun in the water as any person I have known. You didn't have to throw a stick in the water to get him to go in. Of course, he would bring back a stick to you if you did throw one in. He would even have brought back a piano if you had thrown one in.

That reminds me of the night, way after midnight, when he went a-roving in the light of the moon and brought back a small chest of drawers that he found somewhere—how far from the house nobody ever knew; since it was Rex, it could easily have been half a mile. There were no drawers in the chest when he got it home, and it wasn't a good one—he hadn't taken it out of anybody's house; it was just an old cheap piece that somebody had abandoned on a trash heap. Still, it was something he wanted, probably because it presented a nice problem in transportation. It tested his mettle. We first knew about his achievement when, deep in the night, we heard him trying to get the chest up onto the porch. It sounded as if two or three people were trying to tear the house down. We came downstairs and turned on the porch light. Rex was on the top step trying to pull the thing up, but it had caught somehow and he was just holding his own. I suppose he would have held his own till dawn if we hadn't helped him. The next day we carted the chest miles away and threw it out. If we had thrown it out in a nearby alley, he would have brought it home again, as a small token of his integrity in such matters. After all, he had been taught to carry heavy wooden objects about, and he was proud of his prowess.

I am glad Rex never saw a trained police dog jump. He was just an amateur jumper himself, but the most daring and tenacious I have ever seen. He would take on any fence we pointed out to him. Six feet was easy for him, and he could do eight by making a tremendous leap and hauling himself over finally by his paws, grunting and straining; but he lived and died without knowing that twelve- and sixteen-foot walls were too much for him. Frequently, after letting him try to go over one for a while, we would have to carry him home. He would never have given up trying.

There was in his world no such thing as the impossible. Even death couldn't beat him down. He died, it is true, but only, as one of his admirers said, after "straight-arming the death angel" for more than an hour. Late one afternoon he wandered home, too slowly and too uncertainly to be the Rex that had trotted briskly homeward up our avenue for ten years. I think we all knew when he came through the gate that he was dying. He had apparently taken a terrible beating, probably from the owner of some dog that he had got into a fight with. His head and body were scarred. His heavy collar with the teeth marks of many a battle on it was awry; some of the big brass studs in it were sprung loose from the leather. He licked at our hands and, staggering, fell, but got up again. We could see that he was looking for someone. One of his three masters was not home. He did not get home for an hour. During that hour the bull terrier fought against death as he had fought against the cold, strong current of Alum Creek, as he had fought to climb twelve-foot walls. When the person he was waiting for did come through the gate, whistling, ceasing to whistle, Rex walked a few wabbly paces toward him, touched his hand with his muzzle, and fell down again. This time he didn't get up.

After reading Thurber's story, I direct students to draw a giant "T" on a sheet of paper. On the left-hand side of the "T", students list the various traits of Thurber's dog, as revealed in the story: "brave," "determined," etc. On the right-hand side, students describe an anecdote from the story that illustrates and reveals that trait:

Trait	How is it revealed?
1. brave	1. dives into Alum Creek from a height of 10 feet.
2. determined	2. tries to jump 12-foot walls
3. etc.	3. etc.

The next step is for students to create and organize their notes and information for their own character sketch. One way to do this is to create a second giant "T", this time listing the traits of their chosen character on the left side and a brief summary of the illustrative anecdotes they'll use on the right side. If done conscientiously, these notes and this structure will make the actual writing of the character sketch much easier since all the ideas have been generated ahead of time.

Some of my students write character sketches of their parents or one of their friends or teachers. Others follow Thurber's model and write a sketch of their pet. This is what I did in the following example:

> His name was "Muggsy." At least, that's what my niece told us when she brought the month-old puppy to us one summer. "What a dumb name!" I thought. Surely we can do better than THAT. Let's name him Johann Sebastian Bark or Dwight D. Eisenhowl or Paw Newman. How about Christian Diog or Virginia Woof or Edgar Allan Paw or Pierre Cardog? But, by the time I had settled on a really GOOD name, "Barkley," we had had the puppy for a week and he was responding quite happily to—of all the names—"Muggsy." So, "Muggsy" it was; "Muggs" when we were in a hurry to call him; and "Muggers" to our neighbors.
>
> Muggsy was small as a puppy—tiny, in fact. We had no idea how big he would become since we had never really seen an adult cockapoo before. When we first allowed Muggs to come into our bedroom at night, he dashed under the bed and curled up there, ready to sleep. He was so small as a puppy that he barely needed to duck his head as he walked under the bedframe. Every night from then on, Muggsy would sleep under the bed but, while the opening between the floor and the bedframe remained the same size, Muggsy did not. As a fully-grown adult, then, Muggs would approach the bedframe, flatten himself against the floor, extend his back legs fully behind him, and inch and crawl and slide his way under the bed. It was a tight squeeze every time, but Muggs never seemed to mind.
>
> At one time we thought we would send Muggs to obedience school and make him "new and improved." There was even a conveniently scheduled series of classes being offered by the local YMCA. Of course, Muggs' father—that's me—had to go with, and be trained right along with him. Maybe that was the problem: we both flunked the class.
>
> We didn't mean to, of course. It wasn't OUR fault. But look at the problems we faced: one of the exercises each week, for instance, had us all walking in a circle around this huge gymnasium. Fine! But walking just behind me was a full-grown Dober-

man Pinscher who constantly strained to move forward and get closer to me. I knew what he was doing, you see. He was eyeing my backside and thinking, "Oh, good! Lunchtime!"

Whenever I walked in that circle, then, Muggsy could not keep up with me. I moved fast, always trying to get more than a jaw's length away from the Doberman. It was "Walk or be eaten" and Muggsy would just have to watch out for himself.

The Doberman wasn't the only problem, either. There was also Gertie, an elderly woman who served as the instructor's assistant. The instructor himself was a pleasant-enough person who stood in the center of our large circle and gave directions and guidance. The enforcement of his directions, however, was left to Gertie, and she did her job well. One time, for example, we were told to have our dog sit, then gently tug on the leash to get the dog back up and walking again. I guess my tugs were TOO gentle: Muggsy remained sitting, barely bothering to look up at me with those eyes that said, "Was there something you wanted, perchance, or is there a breeze in here?"

Unfortunately, at that moment Gertie saw us. Everyone else was by now up and moving, but not Muggs. He was planted on the floor, seriously considering taking a nap as a suitable way to pass the time. Well, Gertie stomped over to us, grabbed the leash from my hands, and yelled, "No, no, here's how to do it!" She yanked on the leash with a force that all but separated Muggsy's furry head from his body. Muggs wasn't only UP, he was now three inches longer than he had been before. He choked, gasped, and struggled for air as Gertie handed me back the leash with a triumphant "See how it works?"

Oh, yes, I saw. And so did Muggs. From that time on in class, all Gertie had to do was glance in Muggsy's direction—no matter how far away she was, even if it was across the whole length of the gymnasium—but establish that eye contact for an instant—and Muggs would simply piddle on the floor in terror. Every time. After the fourth or fifth piddle, I thought "Who needs this?" and withdrew Muggs and his father from the class. We were both relieved.

So Muggsy, the obedience school dropout, was never properly trained, but he was still a delight. He settled into certain routines and became as much a part of our family as our own children. He had to take baths just like our own children—though our own kids didn't jump out of the tub and run dripping wet through every room of the house, crouching behind sofas, bouncing off beds, racing upstairs into the kitchen and hitting the vinyl floor at 35 MPH and skidding across it to slam into a cabinet drawer. No, our kids didn't do all this; but Muggsy did. Our kids didn't need 7 towels to dry themselves, either.

Muggsy had some strange habits. No matter how late at night I walked him around the block so he could piddle good-night to his favorite bushes, he would always want to go out again—at 3 in the morning—every morning. But there was a problem: Dad was asleep at 3 A.M., and Dad always seemed to be the only one who knew how to open the front door. What to do? Muggsy solved this dilemma by crawling out from under the bed, trotting over to my side, and sticking his nose in my ear. And then he'd snort. You'd wake up pretty quick, too, if some beast shoved his cold, wet nose in your ear and then blew out the contents of his dripping nostrils. And then Muggsy would stand back a few steps and survey his handiwork. Was I awake now? Or did I need another blast from the pest?

We miss Muggsy now. He isn't with us anymore. About 5 years ago, he developed epilepsy, and the first few seizures were frightening. The doctor gave us pills to control the problem, and that worked pretty well ... for awhile. But then the seizures came again, lasting longer and occurring more frequently. We couldn't go on like this.

On the last day, my wife took Muggs to the vet one more time. She had made an appointment in advance for this particular visit. She waited in the front as the vet took the leash and led Muggs gently into the back room. A few minutes later, the vet returned—alone this time—carrying Muggsy's leash and collar. He was gone, and we still miss him.

When the students assemble in small groups to read and evaluate their rough drafts of this assignment, they should focus on the anecdotes they use in their sketches to illustrate their characters' various traits. Are the anecdotes appropriate and relevant? Are they indeed illustrative of the particular feature that the author wants to show? Some problems for students to watch out for include a tendency to get sidetracked and write a "Personal Experience" paper in which an incident is narrated, but the point of the narrative is lost. The author doesn't make clear what this incident reveals about the character being described and profiled. Another problem arises when students work under the mistaken notion that "more is better" and try to write up every anecdote they can remember about their subject. Three or four pertinent, vivid examples, each illustrating a different facet of the subject's personality, should result in a well-written, interesting composition.

"The Mysteries of Harris Burdick"

One day in my writing class, thirty seconds before the bell was to ring to signal the start of the period, a student rushed to my desk with a book in her hand and said excitedly, "Here! Look at this!" She shoved the book at me and told me to read it right now.

"But the class is about to start," I protested.

"It won't take long. Just look at it!" she begged.

I opened the book, Chris Van Allsburg's *The Mysteries of Harris Burdick* (1984) and began turning the pages. She was right: it didn't take me long at all to read it since each page featured only a drawing accompanied by a single line from a story. But, what lines! One page showed a drawing of two circles of light, like fireflies, hovering over a sleeping boy, and the accompanying story line: "A tiny voice asked, 'Is he the one?'" Another single story line stated, "It all began when someone left the window open." Each page and each line was exciting, leading readers to wonder what was happening and inviting them to fill in the rest of the missing story with information and fantasies from their own imagination.

Ever since my first introduction to it, I have shown this book to each of my writing classes, and the response is always the same: students ask if they can write a story using one of the "Harris Burdick" lines as a stimulus. Sometimes the line is used at the beginning of the students' stories; other times it is embedded in the middle or near the end. But as story starters, the "Harris Burdick" lines are exciting, leading students to work enthusiastically on narrative writing.

Something else that students have done with the "Harris Burdick" lines is to create single lines of their own. I tried it myself and enjoyed the word-play and the struggle to create something suspenseful and exciting and intriguing. The examples below are some of the best ones that my students and I produced:

The Time Machine

In the front window, he saw the future; in the back window, he saw the past. But he couldn't believe what he saw in the side window.

—Corinthia

The Choice

In front of him was a big board with three flashing buttons, red, yellow, and blue. Which one was the <u>right</u> one?

—Melissa

The Visit

It left as suddenly as it had come, and the people stood in wonder at what it had left behind.

—Robin

After Midnight

She felt its presence again even before she turned around.

—Laurie

She adjusted the microscope and gasped at what she saw.

—Jessica

A look of horror washed across his face as he peered into the enormous yellow eyes.

—Zan

She stared at the building across the street. Two hours before, the lot had been empty.

—Alison

He watched in horror as his image slowly disappeared from the mirror.

—Andy

You might have your students write their own "Harris Burdick" lines and then type up the best ones, hand them out to the class, and invite students to use one of them as a stimulus for story writing. Some of the best stories my students have written have been produced this way.

Punctuating Dialogue

For many of the preceding activities, students will be using dialogue between characters as a way to reveal personality and move the action along. This is an appropriate time, then, to teach students how to punctuate dialogue correctly. Type up a passage from a story that contains a fair amount of dialogue, *but omit all the punctuation.* I have used a simple children's story from the book *Frog and Toad All Year* by

Arnold Lobel (1976). This following passage is from "Down the Hill," one of the stories in the book. First the original:

> Frog knocked at Toad's door. "Toad, wake up!" he cried. "Come out and see how wonderful the winter is."
> "I will not," said Toad. "I am in my warm bed."
> "Winter is beautiful," said Frog. "Come out and have fun."
> "Blah!" said. Toad. "I do not have any winter clothes."
> Frog came into the house. "I have brought you some things to wear," he said. Frog pushed a coat down over the top of Toad. Frog pulled snowpants up over the bottom of Toad. He put a hat and scarf on Toad's head.
> "Help!" cried Toad. "My best friend is trying to kill me."
> "I am only getting you ready for winter," said Frog. Frog and Toad went outside. They tramped through the snow. "We will ride down this big hill on my sled," said Frog.
> "Not me," said Toad.
> "Do not be afraid," said Frog. "I will be with you on the sled. It will be a fine fast ride. Toad, you sit in front. I will sit right behind you." . . . (4–8)

And now the same passage, again, but with all the punctuation removed:

> Frog knocked at Toads door Toad wake up he cried come out and see how wonderful the winter is I will not said Toad I am in my warm bed winter is beautiful said Frog come out and have fun blah said Toad I do not have any winter clothes Frog came into the house I have brought you some things to wear he said Frog pushed a coat down over the top of Toad Frog pulled snowpants up over the bottom of Toad he put a hat and scarf on Toads head help cried Toad my best friend is trying to kill me I am only getting you ready for winter said Frog Frog and Toad went outside they tramped through the snow we will ride down this big hill on my sled said Frog not me said Toad do not be afraid said Frog I will be with you on the sled it will be a fine fast ride Toad you sit in front I will sit right behind you. . . .

This editing activity might be presented to the students at any time during the narrative writing unit, but it is especially pertinent and helpful if the students engage in this exercise just prior to their drafting of a paper which requires the use of dialogue.

"Draw an Island"

Creative dramatics and art projects can also serve as appropriate and valuable prewriting activities for narrative writing. In this next series of experiences, student-made drawings are utilized for motivation:

Step 1: Have plenty of sheets of construction paper and colored felt pens on hand for this exercise. Announce the following directions to the class:

  a. "Draw an island using the materials provided. The island may be of any size or shape."

  b. "Give your island a name: 'Basketball Island,' 'Skull Island,' etc., reflecting its shape or characteristics." [One of my students traced her hand on the paper and called the result "Five-Finger Island."]

  c. "Identify and draw landmarks on your island: mountains, rivers, caves, valleys, waterfalls, forests, etc."

Place the finished products on the walls of the classroom for all to see.

Step 2: "Imagine that you are stranded on your island. You might have been there for only a few days, or perhaps you have been there for several years. Write a five-day diary of your adventures. You may choose to write about any five days of your confinement on the island (the day you arrived, the day you discovered the Valley of the Dinosaurs, etc.), but write only one entry each day during the next five days of class."

If you wish, you might add more specific directions for each day's entry, such as:

  a. "Today, try to work into your entry a description of how you arrived on the island." (skills: flashback, exposition)

  b. "A natural disaster occurs on your island (a tidal wave, an earthquake, a fire, etc.). Describe the events as they proceed, and tell how you survived the disaster." (skill: building suspense)

  c. "Tell about the day you met another person or group of persons on your island. What did you talk about?" (skill: using dialogue)

The list of variations is endless and is limited only by your own and your students' imagination.

"Land of the Giants"

This is a variation on the preceding activity. Before having the students draw their maps of their island, you might have them engage in the following exercise, which will give an interesting twist to their subsequent writing.

Assemble students in small groups of four or five. Set up the situation by announcing,

> "Your group is in the 'Land of the Giants.' This is a place in which everything around you is of gigantic proportions. A pencil is as big as a telephone pole, for instance. Prepare a scene to act out in which you perform a simple activity in this 'Land of the Giants.' You might make a sandwich, dial a telephone, brush your teeth, type a letter—the choice of activity is yours. But decide how you will perform your actions; rehearse your skit; and present it all in pantomime. No talking should occur during the action."

Allow 20 to 30 minutes for students to practice and prepare, and then have each group perform their skit in turn. If the groups have prepared well, then the rest of the class should be able to guess through the performance what the activity is without the group having to announce in advance that "We are going to be trying to drive a car," for instance.

After this introductory exercise, proceed with the map-drawing activity as above, but tell the students that "The island you are going to draw is this 'Land of the Giants.'" The creative dramatics exercise involving the pantomiming of a simple action will have served to give students a vivid idea of what this island environment is like.

Note

1. For an excellent resource to further develop the skill of "showing, not telling," see Caplan (1984).

Works Cited

Caplan, Rebekah. 1984. *Writers in Training: A Guide to Developing A Composition Program for Language Arts Teachers.* Palo Alto: Dale Seymour.

Lobel, Arnold. 1976. "Down the Hill." In *Frog and Toad All Year,* 4–8. New York: Harper & Row

Thurber, James. 1945. "Snapshot of a Dog." In *The Thurber Carnival,* 122–25. New York: Harper & Row.

Van Allsburg, Chris. 1984. *The Mysteries of Harris Burdick.* Boston: Houghton-Mifflin.

8 Speaking of Literature

How one deals with literature in the classroom depends upon one's assumptions and objectives. Imagine, for example, that a ninth-grade English class is about to read and study William Golding's novel *Lord of the Flies* (1955). A teacher who subscribes to the "heritage" approach will be teaching this novel because he or she believes that it is a great work of literature and should therefore be "passed on" to students as part of their education and literary heritage. The instructional emphasis, then, will be on the transmission of information and insights so that the students might suitably appreciate this novel as a major literary work. E. D. Hirsch operates according to this belief and approach in his book *Cultural Literacy* (1987) recommending certain specific terms and literary works that he feels should be transmitted to students as a basic part of their education as students and citizens.

A second, "skills-oriented" approach to the study of *Lord of the Flies* might involve the teacher's concentration on the practice and improvement of certain discrete reading skills. Golding's novel serves this "skills" approach because of its frequent use of symbolism, and a teacher might focus on the identification of these symbols as one of the reading skills to be developed.

In contrast to these instructional methods, an "interactive" approach focuses neither on the transmission of information nor on the mastery of discrete skills. Instead, this approach sees English as dealing with the construction, comprehension, negotiation, and communication of *meanings*. Golding's novel, then, serves as an appropriate vehicle for this meaning-making activity because of its openness to multiple interpretations. Ben Nelms wrote of this characteristic of good literature in his book *Literature in the Classroom: Readers, Texts, and Contexts*, comparing the text to "a construction site" or "the blueprint around which all the activity at a construction site is centered, or the excavation and foundation work upon which the building is to be erected." He continues:

> If the text is simple and direct, each of us may succeed without much ado to erect a house and, as in many American subdivisions, all of the houses built by readers from the same blueprint may look pretty much alike. But if the text is more demanding and if the resulting structure is to be more impos-

ing, the construction site may prove to be a beehive of communal activity, with crane operators, steeplejacks, bricklayers, carpenters, plumbers, interior decorators, landscape artists, and window washers all contributing their bit: an insight here, a relevant piece of information there, and occasionally a sense of direction or an organizing principle. (1)

Dealing with literature in an interactive classroom involves engaging in the whole range of critical thinking skills, including analysis, synthesis, and evaluation. The goal is not to lead students to come up with the one correct answer, but instead *to make students responsible for their own meanings.* Extending Nelms's analogy, we encourage students to construct their own buildings—to create their own meanings—from the text they are given as a blueprint, but at the same time, they must be able to defend their building as a worthwhile creation. So, when a student makes an interpretation of the text, he or she must also answer the follow-up question, "How do you know?" This ties the student to the text and keeps the interpretation from wandering into a bizarre or untenable position.

A lot of classroom talk is involved as a way for students to try out ideas and construct and negotiate meanings—talk in pairs, in small groups, and as a whole class. As the teacher, I certainly want *every* student to talk at some time during our whole-class discussions, but I also want to maintain a positive classroom climate. So I have adopted a practice for conducting class discussions, a procedure that I communicate to my students on the first day of class in September and maintain throughout the year: I will not call on a student to speak; instead, he or she must volunteer to make an oral contribution to the discussion. This is a real compromise since I want all students to participate, but I am at the same time creating a condition whereby a student may successfully choose to remain silent. The reason for this practice is to enable students to feel "safe" in the classroom, to allow *them* to retain control over when they will speak. It is *my* job to create the necessary positive climate that will make the students feel comfortable and willing to contribute. Simply calling abruptly on a student to speak does not mean that suddenly he or she has something to say. There is a reason for the student's silence: she may have nothing to say at this point; he may feel intimidated or uncomfortable; or the student may simply be listening to follow the discussion and learn from others. Too often, the practice of calling on students is used as a weapon to make sure they are paying attention and to punish those who are not. At the beginning of each whole-class discussion, I remind students of the procedure we will follow: "If you have something to say, simply raise your hand briefly, even while a classmate is talking. I will write down your name, and then I will let you know through eye contact that your name has been added to the list of persons who wish to speak. Then you can put down your hand, and I will be sure to call on you when your turn comes." One advantage of this procedure is that it allows students to concentrate on what is being said by others. Their desire to speak is duly noted and their names are written down, so they don't have to sit there with their hands in the air, focusing more on when they will be called upon rather than on the discussion at hand. In addition, this procedure is *fair*, a feature that is very important to students. The students are called upon in the order in which they indicate a desire to speak; and there are no interruptions. Everyone knows who has been recognized to speak and that each person's chance will come in turn to make a contribution.

So, how many students choose to talk under these conditions? Since they know that they will not be called on to speak unless they raise their hand, students might well elect to remain silent and let the one or two outgoing class members do all the talking. The number of students who choose to participate depends a lot on the "openness" of the topic under discussion. If a teacher plays the game "Guess What's in My Mind," a restrictive, controlled form of questioning in which he or she tries to have students verbalize a preconceived answer, then not much discussion at all will be generated or maintained. But if the goal of the discussion is to have students create and negotiate meanings and interpretations of a text, then students are more likely to participate actively and frequently. Once the students realize that the teacher is not going to jump in and save them with "The Right Answer," then they will be much more likely to offer their own interpretations in an attempt to come up with a meaning that makes sense to them. The teacher's function in this kind of dialogue is to make students responsible for their own meanings, to continually ask "How do you know?" in response to an interpretation. This prompts students to refer to the text under discussion for support.

But sometimes there are students who decline to participate at all. Their silence becomes noticeable by the complete absence of any hand raising, despite several days of classroom dialogue. So I have devised a supplemental procedure to involve these particular students: At the beginning of the period, I approach one of the "silent" students privately with this request: "Give me permission to call on you today. If you approve this arrangement, you must understand that you can't take back the permission halfway through the period—the permission extends for the entire class time today. But it also *ends* at the end of the period, so if I want to call on you tomorrow, I will have to get your permission again." Some interesting things happen when I approach students with this suggestion: first, most of the "silent" students are quite willing to grant this permission. For those who decline, I simply say, "That's okay. Let me ask you again tomorrow and see if you feel differently then." But the majority of students I approach this way accept my arrangement. And so, two or three times during the classroom dialogue, I will turn to the student and ask for his or her opinion on the subject at hand. Second—and the most intriguing phenomenon of all—after I have called on this student perhaps two or three times, the student suddenly starts volunteering on his or her own! I'll look up and see the student's hand in the air, so I'll quietly write down the student's name on the list of students who have indicated a desire to speak. And third, this sudden, voluntary participation on the part of the formerly silent student continues to grow in frequency on subsequent days. In this manner, I have encouraged several "silent" students involved in these whole-class discussions, simply by approaching them privately one at a time and offering them this arrangement. I think they appreciate the respect shown them by my asking for permission to call on them instead of my exhibiting a more conventional attitude of "Since you won't volunteer on your own, I'm going to call on you whether you like it or not." Through this arrangement, the students are able to retain control over their involvement by exercising their choice of whether or not to participate.

So, what do students talk about when they're "speaking of literature" in this way? Here are some activities I have used that invite students to do a lot of talking . . . and writing.

Speaking of Poetry

An important goal when discussing and analyzing poetry in class is to make students responsible for their own meanings. Students should be able to create and explain their own meaning for a poem, support their interpretation with references from the text, and respond intelligently to their classmates' perceptions and interpretations. Such competence, however, does not develop when the students are forced to discover a predetermined meaning imposed on the poem by the teacher.

Asking questions about poetry is important, but it is the students who should be asking the questions as they seek to construct meanings. They should then collaborate with classmates to articulate their responses to those questions. The following activity provides a structure for this process.

Introduce a poem to the class by first reading it aloud. Immediately ask students to write down three questions they have about the poem. These can be questions about a certain word ("What does this word mean?" "Why does the poet use this word here?"), a phrase, or a whole section. After the questions have been written, direct the students to form themselves into small groups, with four or five people in each group. Then instruct the students to work within their groups to generate answers to their questions.

This procedure has several advantages over a more traditional, teacher-led discussion: students are encouraged to ask their own questions of the poem instead of simply responding to the teacher's questions; this process uses students' talk as a vehicle for learning, allowing students to try out emerging ideas on each other; and a collaborative approach is used to generate individual meanings and insights.

At the end of the small-group discussions, a recorder appointed for each group should summarize for the whole class what questions were brought up and what responses were generated. The entire class might then work together to provide additional responses and interpretations for those questions that a particular group found difficult to handle. You should find, at the end of this process, that the students will have covered—or more importantly, "*un*covered"—most of the points and parts of the poem that you, the teacher, would have discussed anyway. And they will have done it in a way that makes sense to them and allows them to make sense of the poem.

Sometimes students can respond to a poem, not by analyzing it, but by *imitating* its structure and content. One poem that invites this kind of response is William Stafford's "Fifteen":

Fifteen*

South of the Bridge on Seventeenth
I found back of the willows one summer
day a motorcycle with engine running
as it lay on its side, ticking over
slowly in the high grass. I was fifteen.

I admired all that pulsing gleam, the
shiny flanks, the demure headlights

---

fringed where it lay; I led it gently
to the road and stood with that
companion, ready and friendly. I was fifteen.

We could find the end of a road, meet
the sky on out Seventeenth. I thought about
hills, and patting the handle got back a
confident opinion. On the bridge we indulged
a forward feeling, a tremble. I was fifteen.

Thinking, back farther in the grass I found
the owner, just coming to, where he had flipped
over the rail. He had blood on his hand, was pale—
I helped him walk to his machine. He ran his hand
over it, called me good man, roared away.

I stood there, fifteen.

After reading the poem aloud, discuss the structure and content. Notice that in the first stanza, the speaker in the poem simply reports an incident: he finds an overturned motorcycle by the side of the road. In the second stanza, he responds to the look and feel of the machine, and in the third stanza he begins to imagine and fantasize about what it might be like to own and ride it. The events in the last stanza, however, bring him back sharply to reality.

Invite students to write a poem that imitates this structure, but have them change the *age* of the character, for instance:

Ninety

In the nursing-home cafeteria during lunch-time, I gazed out the window at a group of school-children running and playing "Follow-the-Leader" in the distant meadow. I was ninety.

I loved their laughter and the way they ran in circles and jumped and fell down and then got up again to run some more. They were having a *lot* of fun. I was ninety.

I could lead those children on a merry chase and play "Hide-'n-Go-Seek" and tell stories just like I did so many years ago. I want to do that again. I was ninety.

Turning away from the window at last, I found that my mashed potatoes were cold and hard and the gravy was lumpy. But it was okay. I couldn't finish them anyway because the nurse came up to me and said that lunch-time was over and it was time for me to be wheeled back to my room.

I sat there, ninety.

Notice how the imitation follows the same structure as the original, imitating the progression of the character's thoughts and contrasting those feelings and fantasies with the reality of the situation in the last stanza. Another imitation, this one written by a student, has an interesting twist at the end:

Five

I was playing in the yard. It was sunny and I built a neat-o sandcastle in my sandbox. I could see the older kids waiting for the schoolbus for kindergarten. I was five.

I wanted to play with them. They were so lucky because they were six and they got to go to school with all of their friends. The bus came, so I stood and ran to the fence. "Hey! What about me?" I was five.

If I could go, I'd show them. I'd play with all the toys and meet new friends. I could be just like all the other kids. Still, I was five.

The bus left without me. The bus-driver didn't even wave. Then I could hear my mom calling me. She told me to stay away from the fence. So I turned back to my sandbox.

I kicked my stupid old sandcastle. I hate being five.

—Ron

Another poem that lends itself to imitation is "April" by Marcia Lee Masters (1944), a celebration of that month that is filled with vivid, characteristic images, as you'll notice in the first stanza[1]:

It's lemonade, it's lemonade, it's daisy.
It's a roller-skating, scissor-grinding day;
It's gingham-waisted, chocolate flavored, lazy,
With the children flower-scattered at their play.

Invite students to imitate this first stanza but have them change the *month.* A student who writes about "December," then, would not use the image, "It's lemonade, it's lemonade . . .", but might change it to something more appropriate: "It's Santa Claus, it's Santa Claus, it's holly." By substituting images appropriate for the month they have selected, students come to see both the structure and craft involved in the original. Here is a more complete sample imitation:

October

It's pumpkins, it's pumpkins, it's leaves.
It's a costume-wearing, monster-making fright.
It's rainy-weathered, cloudy-covered, freezing,
With the homes candy-gathered through the night.

Finally, students can write their own "apology," imitating William Carlos Williams's poem "This Is Just to Say." First the original:

This Is Just to Say[**]

I have eaten
the plums
that were in
the icebox

and which
you were probably
saving
for breakfast

Forgive me
they were delicious
so sweet
and so cold.

And now a sample imitation:

This Is Just to Say

I have looked at
the math problems
that were in
your notebook

and which
you had certainly
worked hard on
to arrive at the answers.

Forgive me
they were needed
so easy to get to
and so correct.

Making sense of poetry is a meaning-making process, and the above activities can help in this effort. They involve students in asking questions about poems, constructing appropriate and insightful responses in collaboration with classmates, and imitating the structure and content of poems. Through these activities, students make sense of poems in ways that make sense to them.

Comparing a Poem and a Short Story

To introduce Ray Bradbury's short story "There Will Come Soft Rains" (1965 [1950]) to the class, I describe a few of the author's other works

---

**From *William Carlos Williams: Collected Poems, 1909–1939*. Vol. I. Copyright © 1938 by New Directions Publishing Corp. Reprinted by permission of New Directions.

of science fiction, and then I read the story aloud to the class. In a subsequent whole-class discussion, students ask questions about the story, and their classmates give responses and interpretations. Then I mention that I think we should look closer at a certain part of the story, specifically at the poem that was read to Mrs. McClellan in the library by the mechanical voice. I hand out copies of that poem, "There Will Come Soft Rains" by Sara Teasdale, and read it aloud. More student questions, this time about the poem, and more responses. To focus students' attention on Teasdale's point of view and intent in writing the poem, I direct students, working in pairs, to draw a giant "T" on their paper, dividing the paper into two columns:

The left-hand column is headed "What Is the Poem About?" and students are instructed to list as many topics as they think are appropriate. Then, the students label the right-hand column, "What Is the Author Saying about It?" and for each of the items listed on the left side, students fill in the right-hand side with whatever insights they generate with their partner. Sometimes students will find that they have nothing to say in the right-hand column about a topic they listed on the left side. In this case, they simply erase that item. After about 15 minutes, the written responses are shared with the whole class.

All the preceding discussion of the story and the poem and the activity with the "T" has prepared students to answer the final question: "Why did Bradbury borrow the title of Sara Teasdale's poem for his story?" Another way of getting at the same point is to ask: "How are the story and the poem alike?" I hand out 3 x 5 index cards to each pair of students and instruct them to write their response on the card. Using the cards forces the students to write concisely, to condense their response into a short paragraph. To accomplish this task, students need to choose their words and phrasing carefully. Thus, they need to look closely at exactly what they want to say and how they want to say it. The cards are then collected and read aloud to the class so all students have an opportunity to hear the insights generated by their classmates.

A follow-up to this series of activities that may be worthwhile involves the introduction of a poem that shares some important aspects with Teasdale's, say for example, Carl Sandburg's poem, "Grass," and a comparison of the two works.

Comparing a Poem and a Newspaper Article

Another comparison involves an analysis of the similarities and differences between a poem and a newspaper article in their treatment of a common subject—in this case, an automobile accident. To begin, I hand out copies of the poem "Auto Wreck" by Karl Shapiro:

Auto Wreck***

Its quick soft silver bell beating, beating.
And down the dark one ruby flare
Pulsing out red light like an artery,
The ambulance at top speed floating down
Past beacons and illuminated clocks
Wings in a heavy curve, dips down,
And brakes speed, entering the crowd.
The doors leap open, emptying light;
Stretchers are laid out, the mangled lifted
And stowed into the little hospital.
Then the bell, breaking the hush, tolls once,
And the ambulance with its terrible cargo
Rocking, slightly rocking, moves away,
As the doors, an afterthought, are closed.

We are deranged, walking among the cops
Who sweep glass and are large and composed.
One is still making notes under the light.
One with a bucket douches ponds of blood
Into the street and gutter.
One hangs lanterns on the wrecks that cling,
Empty husks of locusts, to iron poles.

Our throats were tight as tourniquets,
Our feet were bound with splints, but now,
Like convalescents intimate and gauche,
We speak through sickly smiles and warn

***Copyright © William Goyen by arrangement with Wieser & Wieser, Inc., New York.

With the stubborn saw of common sense,
The grim joke and the banal resolution.
The traffic moves around with care,
But we remain, touching a wound
That opens to our richest horror.
Already old, the question Who shall die?
Becomes unspoken Who is innocent?
For death in war is done by hands;
Suicide has cause and stillbirth, logic;
And cancer, simple as a flower, blooms.
But this invites the occult mind,
Cancels our physics with a sneer,
And spatters all we knew of denouement
Across the expedient and wicked stones.

After reading the poem aloud, I invite students to ask questions about the poem—questions about a single word, a particular line, or a whole section. These questions are directed to the whole class that, in turn, attempts to respond with appropriate interpretations and answers. In this way, students work toward the construction of meanings that they find satisfactory. Once the questions stop coming, I introduce the second item—a short newspaper article—that will be compared with the poem:

Man Dies as Vehicle Strikes Pole in Seattle

A 31-year-old man was killed yesterday when the car he was driving went out of control and struck a light pole just east of Seattle. Joe Jones was traveling south on Copley Road about one mile south of Southeast 250th Place when the accident occurred. State patrol officials said Jones had no permanent address.

How are the poem and newspaper article similar? In what ways do they differ in their treatment of the same event, an auto accident? Students are encouraged to look at the different purposes of the two pieces of writing and how that purpose affects the writer's use of language, the details, and the focus. A discussion of how to present these insights in writing brings us to an examination of the different ways to organize a comparison/contrast paper. One might talk first about the poem, identifying the major characteristics of the features, approach, language, etc., and then turn to the news article, pointing out the relevant and respective similarities and differences. Another structure involves moving from one feature or characteristic to another, comparing and contrasting the two items on each point. So one might compare the different purposes of the two pieces of writing and then discuss the similarity or difference in their approach, focus, and tone.

One result of students' completion of this writing assignment is that they come to understand better the purpose of poetry and how it *accomplishes* its purpose. They see that poems do more than simply convey information. Poets look beyond the event at hand to contemplate the significance of such a happening. Students also see that poetry is much more of an "open" text, subject to multiple interpretations, whereas a piece of writing such as a newspaper article or an instruction booklet is aimed at conveying concrete, "closed" facts and a single interpretation as clearly and simply as possible.

These meaning-making activities that engage students with poetry are valuable, but how does one evaluate in the end whether or not students have learned to construct and comprehend meanings on their own? How do students demonstrate that they are now "new and improved" as a result of their participation in these experiences? As a way to assess my students' improved ability, I hand out three poems that the students have never seen before. I read each of them aloud, and then I instruct the students to select *one* of the poems and answer two questions about it in writing: (1) "What is the meaning of the poem for you?" and (2) "How did you determine the meaning?"

The second question is designed to make the students responsible for their interpretation, to encourage them to go back to the text for support. These two questions are appropriate because they require the students to engage in the same kind of thinking and meaning making that they have been doing previously in the whole-class discussions. A competent written response, then, will meet three criteria: it will be *clear, complete,* and *convincing.*

Speaking of Exams

In an interactive classroom, examinations such as the preceding one are used mainly as yet another opportunity to engage students in constructing and communicating meanings and in the metacognitive activities of reflecting and connecting through language. The unusual practice of having students *collaborate* on an exam is actually a desirable strategy in an interactive classroom because of the amount and kind of student talk involved. In order to give a cooperative response to an exam question, students working in pairs or in small groups must negotiate meanings and work to achieve consensus in their response. These are pertinent and valuable skills that a collaborative arrangement can develop. The following are examples of ways to structure an exam so that collaboration—with its emphasis on negotiation of meanings—can occur.

At the end of students' reading of a novel or a play, design an essay test consisting of five or six questions. The students are directed to write on only *one* of those questions, but are given two days for the writing. The specific instructions follow[2]:

> "This is a two-day open-book examination. At the end of the first day, I will pick up your paper and the exam questions, and will hand them back to you at the beginning of class the next day so you can continue writing. The evening of the first day of the exam is a crucial time because you are expected to study your notes and the text, preparing for your second day of writing. If you should find at the end of the first day of the exam that you lack some needed quotes or examples, then use that evening to find that supporting evidence. You might consider getting together with some of your classmates who are writing on the same question, go down to the local pizza palace, and study together."
>
> "Isn't that *cheating*?" a student usually asks at this point.
>
> "No, it's called *learning*," I reply.

This design for an exam results in a "Win-Win" situation: the students win because they have an opportunity to talk to their classmates and strengthen any weaknesses that appear in their essay during the first day's writing; and the teacher wins because the students finish the exam having learned more about the literature or other content than when they started the test.

A similar design for another essay test also uses students' talk as a vehicle for learning and collaboration. Two days before the exam, hand out a copy of the test (containing three to five essay questions) to each student. Announce that, in two days, students will write on *one* of these questions. But they don't know which question it will be. So they may use the next two days in class to "rehearse" possible responses to *each* question with their classmates. On the day of the exam, then, students will enter class prepared to answer any one of the questions. Simply give directions at the beginning of the period on exam day to start writing. Students will ask, "Which question do we have to write on?" And I respond, "I already told you that. You'll write on *one* of them. What I *didn't* tell you is that the choice is *yours*." A little doublespeak in the directions has led the students to learn a tremendous amount in their preparation and rehearsal of responses to *all* of the questions.

Giving Exams Orally

Near the end of the spring semester one year, my ninth-grade students and I had just finished reading and talking about the novel *Lord of the Flies.* It was time for the final exam, so I gave the students a preview of the nature of the test: "The exam will consist of only one question. It will be an open-book test that will last 75 minutes, to be completed in writing." Suddenly a student—one who had participated actively and frequently in our class discussions—asked, "Can we take the test orally?" Immediately three or four classmates expressed a similar interest in this idea. I thought, "Why not?" So I asked, "How many students would be interested in taking the test orally?" Approximately fifteen students raised their hands. It wasn't easy to choose, but I selected seven of the volunteers to try this variation. I didn't want to have all fifteen students participate in this experimental procedure because, if something went wrong for some reason, I wanted to minimize the damage by limiting the number of students who would be affected.

On the day of the exam, the seven students who would take the exam orally went to the library while their classmates completed the test in writing. Since this class was sixth period—the last class of the school day—the seven students would come back to class at the dismissal bell and stay 90 minutes after school for their oral exam.

I handed out the single exam question to the class:

> "Some people say that literature is like a window; others say it is more like a mirror. What do *you* say?"

The students were instructed to support their position with references to the novel they had just read, but they could bring in other literature they had read earlier in the semester, if they wanted. Their written response would be evaluated according to three criteria:

> An "A" paper is *clear:* I can understand exactly what it is they are saying. The writing is articulate, precise, specific.
>
> An "A" paper is *complete:* The writer has covered the subject thoroughly, giving enough examples and explanation that the reader feels satisfied that the topic has been discussed in some depth. One is not left wondering, "But what about . . . ? "The various aspects and angles of the subject have been examined and treated.
>
> An "A" paper is *convincing:* Even if the reader does not agree with the writer's conclusions and interpretation, he or she can understand why the writer feels this way. The reader can see where the interpretation came from; there is adequate, perti-

nent, and substantial support for the position advocated by the writer.

The students wrote on this topic for the entire period, and I collected the papers when the dismissal bell rang. Now it was time to give the same exam orally. The seven students came into class and sat around a rectangular arrangement of tables in the center of the room. Before handing out the exam question, I reminded the students of certain principles and procedures. These pointers were already familiar to the students because of all the class discussions we had held earlier in the semester, but I thought this was a good time for a reminder:

> "When you are given the topic, you will begin working together to create a meaningful response, an interpretation that makes sense to you. It is important for you to understand that the goal is *not* to discover a certain meaning. I am not sitting here with 'The Correct Answer' in my pocket, watching and listening to see if you can guess what that answer is. This is not the case at all. Instead, you are *constructing* an answer, creating an interpretation that is appropriate and meaningful and insightful to all of you.
>
> "This is an exercise in *cooperation,* not competition. I am not evaluating each of you separately, listening for the person who makes the most intelligent statement or gives the longest explanation. The idea is to work *together* to create something meaningful and insightful. The principle you should keep in mind is that 'meaning is not what you start out with but what you end up with.' What is most important, then, is the interpretation and the insight that you have gained at the *end* of your discussion. An analogy might be appropriate here to make this point clear: imagine that I have placed on the table here a large lump of clay, and you are working together to make something creative and clever and practical out of this material. All that matters is what you end up with at the conclusion of your efforts to mold this lump into something meaningful. Until the time when you say that you are finished, you will naturally try out several ideas and variations, accepting some and rejecting others. This is a normal part of the meaning-making process, and you are encouraged to take risks in your deliberations.
>
> "As part of this meaning-making and risk-taking activity, you will find that at times you will disagree with something that one of your classmates has said. It is okay to disagree and to challenge an idea or an interpretation. You are not being rude or disrespectful; instead you are helping the group to create a responsible and worthwhile interpretation. The action of challenging each other to either defend or modify or even abandon an idea is part of this cooperative effort to make sense of the

subject at hand, and you should view these challenges as help-ful instead of hurtful or threatening.

"The last point I wish to make is about how long the discus-sion will last. You realize, of course, that the discussion *has* to end after 90 minutes. That is all the time we have allotted for this exercise. But it might end sooner than that if you and your classmates decide that you have discussed the topic completely and have constructed a meaning that you are entirely satisfied with. Be careful about rushing things: resist a classmate's at-tempt to end the discussion before you have dealt with certain points or perspectives that you feel should be included. But when you begin to feel that you have discussed as much as necessary, check with each other to see how everyone else feels. If you all agree that it is time to close discussion, then, at that point, you are finished, and we will look at the interpretations and insights that you have generated."

After giving this introduction, I handed out the exam question, and the discussion among the students began. I sat off to the side and did not enter into the conversation at any time. It was difficult at times to remain silent. Sometimes I wanted to interrupt to ask, "But what about . . . ?" or to ask a student for textual evidence to support an interpretation that he or she had made. But I simply wrote notes to myself in response to the ongoing dialogue, noting what points were being discussed and what insights were being generated. I also wrote down questions that came to mind and then listened to see if these questions also came up in the discussion for examination.

One aspect of the discussion that I did *not* monitor was the frequency of each student's contributions. This would have been un-fair and manipulative. If I had told the students in advance that their grade depended in part on how *often* they volunteered comments and contributions, I would have inadvertently set up a game in which students vied for chances to speak whether or not they had something worthwhile to contribute. The goal of the whole exercise would have become "Who can speak the most often?" and this was definitely not the direction I wanted the activity to take. Since this was the first time I had attempted an oral exam, I selected seven students who had already demonstrated a willingness to speak frequently. As it turned out, then, all of them spoke often during the oral exam; no one re-mained so restrained or silent that he or she could not share in the grade that the group earned for their efforts.

At the end of the dialogue, I shared with the students my obser-vations about the points they had raised and the depth and insightful-ness of their discussion. The students talked about ways in which literature in general—and *Lord of the Flies* in particular—was both like a window and like a mirror with pertinent examples to illustrate their positions. At one point, a student suggested that perhaps literature is like one of those one-way mirrors that acts *both* as a window and a mirror. An intriguing point. In general, I was impressed with their dialogue: they challenged points raised by others; contributed examples from the text to support their interpretations; and worked cooperatively and sincerely to make sense of the exam question. I found that the same criteria used to evaluate the students' written response to the question—that is, the essay should be *clear*, *complete*, and *convincing*—are appropriate standards by which to assess the quality of the oral discussion.

Notes

1. For the entire poem, see Dunning, Lueders, and Smith (1966, 95).

2. Portions of this discussion on designing exams appeared previously in Golub (1987, 11).

Works Cited

Bradbury, Ray. 1965 [1950]. "There Will Come Soft Rains." In *The Vintage Bradbury*, 322–329. New York: Random House.

Dunning, Stephen, Edward Lueders, and Hugh Smith, eds. 1966. *Reflections on a Gift of Watermelon Pickle . . . and Other Modern Verse.* Glenview, IL: Scott, Foresman.

Golding, William. 1955. *Lord of the Flies.* New York: Coward-McCann.

Golub, Jeff. 1987. "A Design for a Literature Exam." *Washington English Journal* 9.3 (Spring): 11–13.

Hirsch, E. D. 1987. *Cultural Literacy: What Every American Needs to Know.* Boston: Houghton-Mifflin.

Nelms, Ben F., ed. 1988. *Literature in the Classroom: Readers, Texts, and Contexts.* Urbana: National Council of Teachers of English.

Masters, Marcia. 1944. "April." In Dunning, Lueders, and Smith, 95.

Shapiro, Karl. 1978 [1942]. "Auto Wreck." *Collected Poems 1940–1978*, 6. New York: Random House.

Stafford, William. 1964. "Fifteen." In Dunning, Lueders, and Smith, 70.

Williams, William Carlos. 1938. "This Is Just to Say." In Dunning, Lueders, and Smith, 60.

9 Three Interactive Projects

What Does English Deal With?

This is an appropriate activity for an interactive classroom because of its emphasis on the construction of meanings and its use of students' talk in a collaborative arrangement. It invites students to construct a statement on what English deals with. By completing this series of activities, students come to a better understanding of what it is they are studying and doing and learning in their English class, an understanding that is meaningful to them because they have created it themselves.

The activity proceeds in several steps or stages, but individual parts can be used separately if desired. The complete process is especially useful as a final activity at the end of a semester because it allows students to reflect on what they have done throughout the course.

Step 1. Announce to the students that they are going to be given an assignment that requires them to consider exactly what it is that English deals with. Since they have been "doing English" for several years now, it is time to look closely at exactly what it is they have been studying and learning.

"First we need to construct a statement that answers the question, 'What does English deal with?' The statement may be one, two, or even three or more sentences long, but it will be a statement that the whole class has helped to create. Once you have created the statement, then you can use it as a reference for the final writing assignment that follows."

Step 2. "To create this statement about what English deals with, we're going to need words, lots of words: Descriptive, accurate, meaningful words. So let's first create a word bank that we can use to draw upon for the words that we think we might need."

The section of this chapter entitled "What Does English Deal With?" appeared in somewhat different form as Golub, Jeff. 1988. "What Does English Deal With?" *Washington English Journal* 2.1 (Fall): 47–49. Used by permission of *Washington English Journal*.

Form students into six groups of approximately four to five students each. Supply each group with sheets of construction paper and felt pens.

Directions to Groups 1 and 2: "You have 15 minutes to brainstorm nouns that, in your opinion, have something to do with what English deals with. Put down everything you think of; we can eliminate and revise later. But get those words out and down on paper right now." The two groups work independently of each other at this stage.

Directions to Groups 3 and 4: "Brainstorm verbs that, in your opinion, have something to do with what English deals with. . . ." Continue with same directions as given above to Groups 1 and 2.

Directions to Groups 5 and 6: "Write down words that end in *-ing* that have something to do with what English deals with."

Step 3. Direct Groups 1 and 2 to combine their lists, eliminating duplications and creating a final, combined list of the 10 to 15 words that they believe are most descriptive or indicative of what English deals with. The final list, however, must be written in a certain way.

"Write only five of your 'final' words on each sheet of construction paper and allow plenty of blank space between each word." The group might have either two or three sheets of paper at the end of this step, depending on whether they have 10 or 15 words in the final list.

Give these same directions to Groups 3 and 4 and to Groups 5 and 6. They are to combine their lists and create a "final" list of 10 to 15 words. (You will be amazed at the amount—and the quality—of talking that goes on while students are trying to pare down their lists to the 10 to 15 "most important" words.)

Step 4. To prepare for this next activity, tape the final lists from each combined group to the walls around the room. Spread them around; don't put them up all in one place.

"So now you have identified some of the words that you feel are most important in describing what English deals with. But let's not stop here. You might feel that some of these words are still more important than others, and this next activity will allow you to identify those most important words.

"I'm going to hand out to each of you nine of these sticky dots." (You can get several sheets of these dots at any stationery store. Cut them up in advance into groups of nine so you can hand them out quickly.) "You will vote with these dots for those words you feel are the most important words in describing what English deals with. If you want, you can place all nine dots beside one single word; or you can vote for a total of nine different words, if you choose. It's up to you. But when all of you are finished and seated again, you will then have a pretty good idea of which words seem most important because they will have the most dots beside them. Start now."

Step 5. Reassemble the students into their original six groups: "Now we have some words that we can use to construct our statement on what English deals with. Not only do we have a lot of words that we can use, but we also have some idea of which words seem to be most descriptive and important to us.

"Each group should now create a statement. It will take you some time to do this; no problem. What is most important is that your final statement should be one that everyone in the group has helped to construct and that everyone agrees with to a large extent. Feel free to draw from the word bank we have created, but don't feel pressured to do so. It is there only for your information and reference."

This step may take two hours or more to complete.

Step 6 Once each group has drafted a statement, direct a representative from each group to show that statement to another group. The representative from Group 1 consults with the members of Group 2; the representative from Group 2 goes over to Group 3, etc. The purpose of this consulting is to obtain feedback needed for a subsequent revision. The representatives go back to their statements, accordingly.

Step 7. Once again combine the groups: Groups 1 and 2 get together; 3 and 4; 5 and 6. Direct the students to create a single statement among them, using their group statements for reference. They might take one of several actions. For instance, when Groups 1 and 2 get together, they might decide that Group 1's statement is perfectly acceptable as it stands or that Group 2's is the one they want. They might decide to combine the two statements into one, taking the best parts of both for their final product. Or they might decide to draft a whole new statement entirely. This process will also take quite a bit of time, but the talking that goes on is most productive, and the final statements that emerge show a fair amount of insight.

Step 8. To prepare for this final activity, type up all three statements generated by the combined groups (Groups 1 and 2, 3 and 4, 5 and 6). Hand out copies of the statements at the beginning of class.

"Here is what you have so far, and we are now ready to create a single, final statement about what English deals with. Use these statements for reference, but feel free to depart from them if you wish. We are going to work as a single group now, and I hope that each of you will participate at some point to help shape this document that will represent the best thinking of the entire class."

The constructing of this final single statement in both of my ninth-grade classes took one week to complete (5 hours of class time). A different student each day served as the recorder, writing and revising on the overhead projector as the students discussed and argued and shaped the document. At the end of that week, these statements emerged finally from my two classes:

> *English deals with* . . . communication and the development of one's self, and therefore society as a whole. This results from creation and personal interpretation of feelings and ideas.

> *English deals with* . . . a way of teaching people to create and express their ideas through communication using the language to understand each other more clearly.

These were the statements, then, that were used as a reference for the following writing assignment described in Step 9.

Step 9. This exercise is given to the students immediately after the completion of the single-class statement:

> *DIRECTIONS:* Write on only *one* of the following questions:

> *Question 1:* Why is the exercise you just completed (the discussing and composing of a single statement about what English deals with) an appropriate and worthwhile activity for an English class? Use the statement that the class composed to support your ideas and explanation.

> *Question 2:* Perhaps you don't like the single statement that the class put together about what English deals with. That's okay; it's perfectly fine to disagree. In that case, do the following:

> a. Identify the problems or weaknesses of the statement. What's wrong with it?

> b. Create your own statement about what English deals with.

> c. Explain how your statement is better than the other one.

Through this series of activities, culminating in the above writing assignment, students come to a better understanding of exactly what it is they are studying and doing and learning in English. This understanding makes sense to them, moreover, because they have created it themselves. An additional insight occurs when students realize that, in their efforts to construct their statement about what English deals with, they were engaging in the very process they were trying to describe.

"Interview an Expert"

This project is similar to the popular Foxfire project in that students are directed to interview a member of their community. The focus and scope of this activity, however, are sharply defined, making it suitable for use when one has only a limited amount of time to devote to such a unit.

The way in which this project came about for my tenth-grade English class is notable for the amount of student involvement in its design. One weekend, after having read a journal article about the Foxfire project, I thought it might be fun to have my students interview an expert. It sounded like a good idea since it would involve collaborative work, oral communication skills, and other worthwhile language performances. But that was as far as my thinking went. I had no idea how to proceed with this project, how to structure it or make it happen for the students. But, I decided to try it, anyway. So, the next Monday, I simply announced to my class that, for their term project, they would interview an expert.

Silence. A lot of silence.

And then a student raised his hand and asked a question: "An expert in *what?*"

"Good question!" I replied. "Let's create a list of things that one could be an expert in. Leon, will you and Narcis go to the blackboard and write down all the things that your classmates think of?"

And that's what we did for the next 10 minutes: students shouted out contributions in response to this question, and Leon and Narcis wrote them all down on the board as each student copied them so everyone would have this resource list available to them.

And then another question came up: "How will we know if they're really an expert?"

"Good question! Let's make another list, this time of criteria for determining whether or not they're really an expert." And so we did.

And then a third question: "What'll we ask them when we talk to them?" A third list of possibilities was generated and written down.

And then the last question: "How do we present all the stuff we find out?" Once again we brainstormed ways in which students might present their findings: through a written report, a demonstration of a process, photographs, bulletin board display, etc.

The students and I negotiated the deadlines and length of oral presentations, and then I made a suggestion: "You know, it would be a disaster if a student arrived at his or her final presentation, only to have some classmates object that the subject wasn't really an expert at all. What if we scheduled a separate time for each of you to speak to the class and convince us that you have indeed found an expert for your project. Then, when you make your final presentation three weeks later, no one can object because you have already established the credibility of your subject." The students agreed with this plan, and so, two weeks later, each student in turn gave a 5 to 10 minute speech in which they described their subject's background, expertise, awards and experience. It was understood that the class would then respond with questions and comments, at the end of which the class would vote on whether or not they agreed that this was indeed an expert. Another advantage of including this preliminary step is that the students do not have to devote any time or space in their final presentation to the establishment of their subject's credibility; it has already been taken care of.

The final presentations went very well: some students brought in their expert, introduced him or her to the class, and conducted an interview right there, allowing questions from the audience at the end. Other students demonstrated a process they had learned from their expert. And still others presented their findings and interview in a written report. But, throughout the project, the students demonstrated a high degree of enthusiasm and commitment since they had determined much of the structure and design of the activity.

The Great Junk Mail Project

Students need to be able to recognize doublespeak and see it for what it really is: language and other means of persuasion that distort information and deceive the consumer. If students can be made aware of the presence and operation of doublespeak in their world, they can be protected against its persuasive tactics. This sequence of activities will give students opportunities to detect and even practice doublespeak. The unit culminates in a project in which the students, working in pairs or small groups, examine one piece of junk mail, identifying and describing all the doublespeak techniques they can find.

Begin by describing a few examples of doublespeak to orient the students. The NCTE Committee on Doublespeak has prepared some pertinent and valuable materials that can be used for this purpose. And your students will quickly come up with examples of their own. One of my students mentioned that she looked in a jewelry store window and saw a tag on a pearl necklace that declared, "Genuine imitation pearl." A moment's thought about this tag reveals what the jeweler really means—that the necklace is *genuinely* composed of imitation pearls. But the word *genuine* is seductive, leading the consumer to think that this is indeed a *real* pearl necklace. This is doublespeak: language or other means of persuasion that do not lie, but that distort and deceive.

Another example is the use of the phrase "up to 60 percent off" on merchandise to lead the shopper to think that significant bargains are to be found here. But the phrase "up to . . ." is misleading: perhaps one or two undesirable items in the store are indeed marked down by 60 percent, but the rest of the items are still being offered with only a slight reduction in price. You won't know this for sure, of course, until you go into the store and check things out for yourself—and this is what the owners hope will happen as a way to increase the number of shoppers in their store.

Once students become sensitized to the nature and characteristics of doublespeak, instruct each of them to bring in one or two cereal boxes for examination—the more boxes and brands of cereal, the better. Working together in small groups, students should identify all the different forms of doublespeak that are used on the front and back panels of these boxes: the phrase "real fruit taste," for instance, does not mean that there is any fruit at all in the box. They should look at the colors, the use of familiar TV cartoon characters, the drawings, and the offers of contests and prizes. Have each group share their insights with the rest of the class.

The students can also practice creating doublespeak themselves: have them write classified ads for such undesirable items as an old, broken-down shack in the middle of a swamp, trying to make the items sound as attractive as possible ("Waterfront property, close to nature," for instance), or a mean-tempered dog ("Want protection? A feeling of security? Then you want this strong pet with a distinctive mood, a personality that protects and defends. This dog means business, and at a price you can afford").

The students can also write longer pieces of doublespeak, responding to such situations as this one described in the NCTE publication *Ideas for Teaching English in the Junior High and Middle School* (Carter and Rashkis 1980):

> Today was a bad day for you at school. You walked into English class and pushed another kid into the door, causing the boy to get a black eye. You called him a crybaby, pulled his hair, and knocked his notebook on the floor. You stomped to your desk, sat down, and began carving your initials in the wood with your protractor. Mimeograph papers were passed out, and you dropped them on the floor in front of your desk. When the teacher asked you to pick them up, you told her to "cool it." You were sent to the office and on the way out threw your dictionary in the wastepaper basket and slammed the door. Write the story you told the principal. (160)

The final project in this unit involves the students in an examination of all the doublespeak techniques displayed in a piece of junk mail. Working alone or in small groups, students select an item of junk mail that they or their parents have received and analyze the following areas and techniques:

1. *The Envelope.* Are there pictures on the envelope? What are they? What are they designed to do? Any slogans? Other words?

2. *Choice of Words.* Point out examples of words used to make the item seem as attractive as possible. What words are used to describe the product?

3. *Doublespeak Techniques.* Look for weasel words, unfinished comparisons, vague words. Also look for places where they "compliment the consumer" and say, "We're different and unique."

4. *Look at the Pictures.* Do the pictures represent doublespeak? Is the item shown actual size? How do the pictures make the product look appealing and attractive?

5. *How Much Will It Cost?* Look at the order blank. How much exactly will you have to pay to get this item? What exactly are you signing yourself up for if you decide to say "Yes"?

6. *Evaluate the Junk Mail.* In a separate section, give your own opinion about how good a job the advertisers did in trying to sell the product. What did they do that was particularly clever? What did they do that you thought was sneaky or unfair? Even if you are not persuaded to buy the product, do you think that many other people might be tempted?

The students' presentation of their findings can take many forms: some might choose to submit a written analysis while others create a bulletin board display or produce visual materials to accompany their oral presentation to the class. I usually give my students approximately one month to complete this final project, devoting one day each week in class to this task. Students know that they must spend considerable time outside of class preparing their project, but the weekly in-class time gives me a chance to monitor their progress and offer assistance. I have received some incredible projects and presentations in the end, of all sizes and composition, but almost every student who has completed the great "Junk Mail" project says the same thing: "I never realized before how much doublespeak there is. . . ."

Works Cited

Carter, Candy, and Zora M. Rashkis, eds. 1980. *Ideas for Teaching English in the Junior High and Middle School.* Urbana: National Council of Teachers of English.

Golub, Jeff. 1988. "What Does English Deal With?" *Washington English Journal* 2.1 (Fall): 47–49.

10 Computers and English Instruction

Using computers in your class as a tool for English instruction does not mean that you must change your curriculum and start doing something entirely different. Computers are a valuable resource simply because:

1. They provide students with a more efficient means of drafting, revising, editing, and polishing their writing efforts; and

2. They allow students to learn and do things in ways that they could not do otherwise.

In this chapter, I want to describe some ways of using computers to work with students' writing in an English class. An excellent resource for additional activities may be found in the recent NCTE publication, *The English Classroom in the Computer Age: Thirty Lesson Plans* (Wresch 1991). In describing the exercises in this first part, I am going to assume that you and your students have access to a computer lab equipped with enough computers so that each student (or at least, each pair of students) can work at one. In a later section on revising, I'll describe an activity that can be conducted with only a single computer in a classroom.

Invisible Writing

In the beginning stage of writing, it is important that students simply get their ideas and "rough-draft" thoughts down without worrying about spelling or other editorial matters. Sometimes, though, students become overly concerned with editing, and thus the free flow of words is blocked. Stephen Marcus, of the University of California–Santa Barbara, and others have described a technique to overcome this problem[1]: when the students sit down at the computer to write, instruct them to either darken the screen by turning down the contrast or simply turn off the monitor. Either way, the screen should now be hidden from view, and then the students begin writing. It is frustrating initially, of course, since the students cannot see what they are writing (or have written), but it also frees the writers to concentrate on what they are saying without being concerned about matters of style and correctness. Fluency of thought and words can be developed in this way.

A couple of variations are possible: students can write normally (with the screen visible to them), and then, at a certain point, darken the screen and write about (1) "What do I want my reader to care about at this point?" or (2) "What am I worried about in my writing at this point?" This time-out period for reflection may help students focus on the direction of their writing and improve their subsequent work when they return to their drafting effort.

Another variation takes a bit of preparation to set up, but the resulting activity is unusual and even startling for the students: if your lab's computers are situated side-by-side (along the walls, for instance), unplug the cord going from the keyboard to the screen outlet located on the back of the computer. Working with each pair of adjacent computers, plug the keyboard cord from computer "A" into the back of computer "B", and vice versa. Thus, when two students sit at this pair of computers, they will work as a team. As the student seated at computer "A" begins typing, his or her words will appear on the screen of computer "B". Only the student in front of computer "B" will be able to see what student "A" is typing. At any point, student "B" can give feedback to student "A" about the ideas and direction of the drafting effort. As student "B" types his or her response, the words will appear on student "A"'s computer screen. The effect is unsettling at first, but the results may be productive. Students working at the "A" computers develop their fluency since they are engaging in "invisible" writing, and they are also receiving simultaneously valuable feedback and suggestions and insights from their classmates seated at the "B" computer.

Telling Suspenseful Stories

In Chapter 7, I described an activity in which students create their own suspenseful lines for a story, using the lines in *The Mysteries of Harris Burdick* as a model. Such lines—as "He watched in horror as his image slowly disappeared from the mirror" and "She stared at the building across the street. Two hours before, the lot had been empty"—can be used for a writing exercise in which students embed the lines in a short story. Using computers, students can go one step further with this exercise: begin by having students create their own "Harris Burdick" line, typing it at the top of the screen. Students should then drop down one line and create a sentence that could be used as the last sentence of a story. The ending sentence does not have to have anything at all to do with the suspenseful line they created above.

After these two lines have been created, students should move to another computer in the room and fill in the necessary details and description and plot development to connect the two lines that their classmate has created on the screen. As they type, continuing the story from the first, suspenseful line, the ending sentence will simply move to the right and down, maintaining its position as the last sentence of the story. Writing efforts should be shared at the end of the exercise, students listening to see if the writer has indeed created a coherent transition from the first to the last sentence.

A Matter of Style

You will probably recognize the following passage as being from George Orwell's novel *Animal Farm* (1946). First, read the passage, and then we'll do something with it:

> The animals had their breakfast, and then Snowball and Napoleon called them together again.
>
> "Comrades," said Snowball, "it is half-past six and we have a long day before us. Today we begin the hay harvest. We will work very hard, and everyone is expected to contribute their labor to the cause. But there is another matter that must be attended to first."
>
> The pigs now revealed that during the past three months they had taught themselves to read and write from an old spelling book which had belonged to Mr. Jones's children and which had been thrown on the rubbish heap. (32)

You've just read the passage, right? Good. But, before we continue this activity, I must confess something: I lied to you. It's true that this is a passage from *Animal Farm,* but not *all* of it is from the novel. *I created and inserted my own sentence into the above passage.* Can you tell which sentence has been added to the original text? Go back and reread the passage, and pay particular attention to the strategies you are using to try and figure out which sentence is a forgery. Once you have made your choice, turn to end note 2 of this chapter and see if you guessed correctly.[2]

I imagine that, in trying to figure out which sentence I had created myself and inserted into the above passage, you looked at several elements: you probably analyzed the content and meaning of each sentence, trying to see if one sentence was out of place in some way: maybe it didn't move the story or narration or action along; it didn't fit with the surrounding sentences. You probably also looked at the style of writing. Did one sentence stand out because it was too long or too short in comparison with the rest of the text? Was one sentence too wordy or vague while the others were sharp and crisp? What about word choice? Did you examine that aspect? And I'm pretty sure you checked the grammatical elements of each sentence, looking to see if one sentence was awkward in its structure. But, however you went about determining which sentence was the forgery, I *know* that you looked *closely* at that passage.

And I had to do exactly the same kind of textual analysis that *you* did in order to create and insert my sentence: once I had chosen that particular passage for this activity, I had to look closely at the content and meaning of each sentence, trying to make a decision about where in the passage I would insert an additional bit of narration or dialogue. What would I have my sentence say that would sound as if it belonged in that particular place? Did it fit with the sentences before and after? And I chose my words carefully so they wouldn't stand out as different from the rest of the text. I also examined the grammar of my sentence so it wouldn't sound too complex or too simple. That element, too, had to be shaped to fit in with the rest of the passage.

This, then, becomes the point of the exercise: to focus students' attention on matters of style, to have students engage in textual analysis. The general idea for this activity is based on a software program called *Suspect Sentences,* published by Ginn and Company (1986). The program allows students to choose from 60 different passages from popular fiction. The chosen excerpt is displayed on the screen, and students, working alone or in pairs or in larger teams, create and insert their own sentence into the passage. Then another student (or pair or team) tries to determine which sentence in the passage is the forgery.

You do not have to purchase the software program in order to conduct this activity. You can instruct students to select a passage from the novel they are currently reading in class for this exercise, or you can have students choose a passage from a book they are currently reading on their own. On a specified day, students type their selected passage, complete with their own, added sentence, into the computer, and then they move to a classmate's computer to try and detect which sentence is the "suspect" one. Using computers for this exercise allows students to easily insert their sentence anywhere they want in the passage. As they type, the rest of the text simply moves to the right and down to accommodate the additional words. By having students reflect on the strategies they used to detect the forged sentence, you can sensitize them to various matters of style and substance in their reading.

Simulating an Electronic Bulletin Board

This exercise simulates what happens on an electronic bulletin board. Through the use of a computer and a modem, people can log onto an electronic bulletin board or information service such as CompuServe and engage in electronic conversations on a variety of topics. Messages are posted on these boards in response to previously written comments. In some cases, conversations extend over weeks and months with many people taking part. Ideas are shared, argued, and elaborated, each contributor continuing the conversation through relevant statements or observations. It all happens in much the same way as the classroom exercise below, and the exchange of opinions is valuable as a source of ideas and insights. And it is authentic communication, too, involving people writing to a real audience for real purposes.

Begin by having the students write a rough draft of their topic on the computer. When it appears that most students have either finished their draft or have at least written a considerable amount, direct students to stop writing, move to a classmate's computer, read what their classmate has written, and then, two lines below the existing text, write a response. (The students might even change the font or the size of their text to distinguish it from the original writer's text above). In the response, the student should deal only with the content of the essay: he or she may argue or agree with what was said, bring up points that the writer has not thought of, or describe his or her own perspective of the topic under discussion. But, in some way, students should comment on the expressed ideas of the original writer and give the writer something to think about and consider. After writing a response, students should move to still another computer, read what has been written, and add a comment at the end. This time, the student can not only respond to what the original writer has written; he or she can continue or argue the thoughts expressed by the first respondent. The students do not have to move from one computer to another all at the same time. When one student is finished responding at one computer, he or she simply looks around the room to find another computer that is free at that moment. This activity of responding to several comments should continue for most of the period and can even be carried over to the next day's class. At the end of this exercise, all students return to their original computer and read the string of responses that have been added to the end of their draft. In this way, students gain valuable insights and perspectives on their topic that can be considered and included in their subsequent revision.

Revising with a Word Processor

Students enter their English class in September thinking that revising a paper means copying it over in ink. But it's much more than that. "Revising" means literally to "re-see," and one revises by "seeing" the paper again, looking for places where something needs to be added or eliminated or moved around from one place in the paper to another. Perhaps a word or a phrase needs to be taken out and something else substituted in its place. This is revising.

One of the best ways to model this process for students is to use a computer hooked up to an LCD viewer, a device that sits on top of an overhead projector. The viewer enables the overhead to project a wall-size display of the computer screen. In preparation for a modeling session, I will ask a student volunteer to allow me to type his or her draft on the computer for revision by the whole class. On the day of the lesson, then, the students come into class and see Anne's paper projected on a large screen at the front of the room. Anne reads her paper aloud, and then the whole class is invited to offer comments: What works well? What doesn't? What should be added or removed? What should be clarified? Often students will disagree with each other about various points and sections of the paper, but this kind of dialogue is encouraged: "Let Anne hear you talk about the merits of keeping a certain word or about the best way to phrase a certain section. Then she can decide for herself what action to take." I position myself at the computer and take my cues only from Anne since she is the author and is therefore the only one who has the authority to effect a change.

The revising session begins: members of the class offer suggestions of changes to make in various parts of Anne's paper. For every student who says, "Eliminate the part where it says . . .", there is a classmate who argues, "No, I like that part. Keep it in." Anne listens to the arguments and opinions and responses. At last she will turn to me and say, "Okay, here's what I want to do." And only then will I make changes to Anne's paper on the computer. So, in this way, Anne is in total control of her composition at all times. Often within a single class period—with the whole class focused on Anne's paper in this way—the paper undergoes extensive, worthwhile revisions that result in an excellent final copy. The follow-up to this modeling exercise calls for the students to assemble in small groups and spend the next two or three class periods revising each other's draft in the same way that they helped to revise Anne's paper. No further teaching of the revision process is necessary because the students have just experienced what is involved in this phase of writing.

Once in a while a student will object to this procedure because "If I accept their suggestions, then the writing isn't *mine* anymore," a legitimate complaint and a sincere concern. I reply by emphasizing a basic assumption of this exercise and instructional approach: "Writing involves making choices, and *good* writing is knowing the choices that are available to you." This is what this revising exercise is all about—a chance to learn what other choices are available to the author. Often, good ideas come from other people, and the revising talk in small groups encourages these ideas to come out. But it is always up to the author to accept or reject the ideas and suggestions that he or she hears, and this is the second important point I make in response to the student's concern that "The writing won't be mine anymore." In accepting a suggestion for revision, the author is indicating a willingness to accept responsibility for that change, a willingness to stand behind it as a desired and worthwhile improvement. So the language and style (and, indeed, the paper itself) remain the work of the author because, while the suggested change might have come from someone else, the decision to *incorporate* that change rests solely with the author.

Notes

1. The technique of "invisible writing" with a computer was created by Stephen Marcus and is described in detail in Marcus (1991).

2. The inserted line is "We will work very hard, and everyone is expected to contribute their labor to the cause."

Work Cited

Marcus, Stephen. 1991. "Invisible Writing with a Computer: New Sources and Resources." In Wresch, 9–13.

Orwell, George. 1946. *Animal Farm.* New York: Harcourt, Brace & World.

Suspect Sentences. 1986. Lexington, MA: Ginn.

Wresch, William, ed. 1991. *The English Classroom in the Computer Age: Thirty Lesson Plans.* Urbana: National Council of Teachers of English.

11 Talking on the Spur of the Modem

Telecommunications will become one of the most valuable instructional tools of twenty-first-century education. Using a computer and modem, students and teachers can establish connections with other classrooms around the country and around the world. An individual classroom will no longer be defined by four walls and a door. Instead, its boundaries will become as wide as the world itself as students exchange correspondence and perspectives and projects with classmates all over the globe. To get an idea of what will happen with telecommunications in the future, just look at what is happening right now:

- Students at Cold Spring Harbor High School in New York publish each year a school literary magazine entitled *A Vision.* Unlike most school literary magazines, however, this one has a distinctive feature. The 1991–92 edition, for example, has contributions from students in Washington State, Massachusetts, New York, Washington, D.C., China, Spain, Argentina, Australia, Israel, and Russia. Correspondence among the students in these states and countries occurs electronically, some in native languages, with many of the literary contributions submitted electronically to the magazine's student editors in New York.

- Trevor Owen, professor of English education at York University in Toronto, Ontario, runs Writers in Electronic Residence (WIER),[1] a national on-line writing program in Canada. Students compose original works and post them in a computer conference where well-known professional writers join teachers and other students to read and respond to the writing. "Student responses are clearly considered, thoughtful responses" says Owen, noting that students quickly embrace the opportunity to reflect on their experiences as they craft their thoughts in written language: "WIER involves students in a community that is textual in nature. While it is often quite social, especially as the writers and students get to know one another, they have the opportunity to present themselves for what they have to say—in writing—rather than who they appear to be in face-to-face situations."

- Students in a school in Florida collaborated with students in England on a science project. The two groups of students took samples of water from the Hillsborough River in Tampa and the Thames in London and compared water quality and characteristics, hypothesizing about reasons for the differences they found. All correspondence was accomplished electronically through the Computer Pals network run by Malcolm Beazley in Australia.

These projects exemplify and incorporate the features of an interactive classroom: students are actively involved in authentic communication, writing for real audiences and real purposes; they participate in their own learning; they collaborate on projects that engage them in critical thinking and problem solving and decision making.

I want to describe three additional telecommunications projects in detail to give an even better picture of the possibilities available to classroom teachers through this innovative instructional tool. These activities were ones that I was involved in personally while I was teaching at Shorecrest High School in Seattle, Washington.

Homework Hotline

Some years ago I established an electronic "Homework Hotline" on a local area bulletin-board system (BBS) that served students throughout the Greater Seattle area. The Hotline, entitled "Barkley's Classroom" (I was "Barkley") had four conference areas which were described in an introductory message to visitors who logged on to the system:

> Hi! Welcome to Barkley's Classroom. I'm Barkley Woof, a teacher of English, Speech, and writing classes at Shorecrest High School. My classroom here is an electronic meeting place for students, parents, and teachers where you can meet to talk about school and about education in general.
>   My classroom is divided into four areas:
>
>   "Students' Lounge"—A place where students gather to talk about what's happening at school. Visit the lounge, sit down and relax, grab a pop, and join in the conversation.
>
>   "Faculty Lounge"—A place for teachers and administrators to meet and talk and plan together. This is a restricted area, open only to faculty members and other school staff.
>
>   "Parent Conference"—It's always "Open House" for parents in this area of Barkley's Classroom. Ask questions and share concerns about school-related issues as you talk with Barkley and other teachers and parents here.
>
>   "Homework Hotline"—Use the Homework Hotline when you need some help with your English homework or with read-

ing or writing assignments. (I'm an English teacher, remember?). Let me know what you need, and I will do what I can to help you understand and complete the assignment.

The "Students' Lounge" was a place where students from all around the Greater Seattle area could meet electronically and talk by posting and reading messages. Topics and opinions ranged from the serious to the silly, but they tended to cluster around school concerns in general, perhaps because the students realized that they were, after all, in "Barkley's Classroom." I silently eavesdropped on their conversations, but never volunteered my opinion unless addressed directly by a student in a message.

The second conference area, the "Faculty Lounge," was a more private area where teachers and administrators could meet and talk "on the spur of the modem," exchanging notes and ideas and opinions. Access to this area was restricted. An educator who wished to gain access to the "Faculty Lounge" would write me a note of introduction, and then I would inform the BBS system operator that this person should be admitted.

The "Parent Conference" area in "Barkley's Classroom" was the place where parents and other citizens throughout the Puget Sound area could meet and discuss a variety of educational issues among themselves and also with me and other teachers. This conference area really heated up during the Washington State teachers' strike that lasted for two weeks in 1991. Parents posted notes of complaint or support. Questions were asked of me and other teachers. A school board member of one of the local districts joined in the debate. Even students entered the "Parent Conference" area to give their opinions. It was a nice public relations tool.

Another interesting phenomenon that occurred in this particular area of "Barkley's Classroom" was the posting of messages by parents asking me for advice about their child's English class or about education in general. Some parents were confused by a certain instructional approach or by the teacher's requirements for a specific assignment. Others wanted advice about how to motivate their child to read more or even what arguments they could use to persuade their child to stay in school and not drop out. And I'll never forget the debate that raged for an entire month over the benefits or harm of the current grading system used in the schools.

And finally, there was the fourth area of "Barkley's Classroom," the "Homework Hotline" itself. An introductory message that greeted each visitor to this area announced:

> Use the Homework Hotline if you need some help with your
> English homework or with reading or writing assignments. Let
> me know what you need, and I will do what I can to help you
> understand and complete the assignment, although you'll still
> have to do the actual work yourself, of course. I visit my elec-
> tronic classroom at least twice a day (usually in the late after-
> noon and evening), so you will always get a quick reply to your
> questions.

In the "Homework Hotline" area, some students wrote to me for
clarification on assignments their teachers had given; other students
sent me entire compositions they had written for response and editing
help; a few of my own students at Shorecrest High handed in their
homework electronically by sending it to me on the "Hotline."

And then something unexpected began to happen within the
"Homework Hotline" area: students started leaving messages for
other students in general, asking for help with their math and science
and history coursework. Suddenly the "Hotline" became a forum for
peer tutoring in a variety of academic subjects.

The "Homework Hotline" operated for several months, but the
time and energy involved in keeping up with the messages and reading and requests and replies finally became too much. I posted a
message saying that the end of the current semester would signal the
end of "Barkley's Classroom." It was sad to have to terminate such a
project, but I thanked everyone for having shown that such an innovation could work. I envision a time when each school district or county
will operate its own "Homework Hotline" for its students, providing
academic help, answering questions, bringing the students and faculty
and community just a little bit closer to sharing common concerns and
working together toward the improvement of instruction.

AT&T's Learning Network

One of the most fundamental skills for students in the twenty-first
century will be that of information management: how to gain access to
information; how to select appropriate information from an overload
of available resources; how to analyze and evaluate information that
students read, see, and hear daily; and how to communicate one's
conclusions and insights clearly, completely, and persuasively. What
an incredible opportunity is therefore offered to students who participate in AT&T's Learning Network.[2] This program allows students to
practice and develop these information-management skills and to use
them to communicate to real audiences for real purposes.

The Learning Network offers two sessions, one in the fall and one in the spring. The fall session runs from October to December (eleven weeks); the spring session extends from February to May (fifteen weeks). You can participate in either the fall or spring sessions (or both, if you want), and you will be asked on the application form to select one of six curriculum areas that will become the focus of your students' work during the semester. The curriculum choices include:

> Computer Chronicles—develops composition skills, an understanding of language mechanics, and an extended vocabulary through the production of a newspaper on current/local events.

> Mind Works—enhances creative writing skills as students experiment with various forms of expressive writing, such as short stories, poetry, and essays.

> Places and Perspectives—encourages students to explore the history, culture, government and geography of their region and compare it with their distant peers.

> Energy Works—focuses students' attention on how energy needs interact with our environment. Students explore the basic forces of nature by sharing information and experimental observations.

> Society's Problems—enables students to explore and compare situations that confront their respective communities and propose common solutions to these problems.

> Global Issues—stimulates discussions on a range of environmental, social, political, and economic issues that affect the world population. Students are encouraged to propose joint solutions.[3]

When you sign up to participate in the Learning Network, you will be assigned to a Learning Circle composed of six to nine other classrooms around the country (with a couple of the classrooms being located in other parts of the world). Each classroom's teacher in your Learning Circle will have selected the same curriculum area on which to focus their students' efforts throughout the semester.

The students in my debate class took advantage of this opportunity during the fall semester, 1989. We enrolled in the Learning Network and were assigned to a Learning Circle made up of seven other participating classrooms. Five of our electronic partners were from other parts of the United States, and two were from West Germany. Throughout the semester, students and teachers in all eight classrooms exchanged notes electronically with each other through their computers and modems. We introduced ourselves, read about specific reports and projects being prepared by the other classes, participated in surveys, answered questions, and provided information about our region of the country.

During the first week of our electronic exchanges, students from the eight schools introduced themselves by posting messages giving their name and other pertinent information. Some students mentioned their favorite TV shows; others talked of their plans for college or their favorite sports and hobbies. It was interesting to note how many student introductions ended with the request to "Write back soon" or "Hope to hear from you" or "Write back and tell us about yourself." As these messages of introduction came in each day, I posted them on the bulletin board in the back of my classroom and encouraged my students to respond to the students who had written to let them know their messages were received and read. Suddenly students were writing with a definite audience and purpose in mind, establishing connections and making new friends. Two students, for example—one from my class and another from a school in Indiana—discovered from each other's introduction that they shared an interest in collecting guns. Several messages passed between them as they shared information and insights about various aspects of their hobby.

Part of the introductory messages included descriptions of the schools and the surrounding geographical area. My students wrote about Shorecrest High School's marching band being invited to play at President's Bush's inauguration; and we heard, in turn, about some outstanding accomplishments of the other schools in our Learning Circle. We even agreed to exchange "Welcome Packs," a collection of "stuff" from each region. My students assembled and sent such artifacts as a copy of our school newspaper; a few postcards showing such Seattle landmarks as the Space Needle and the Kingdome; a map of Seattle; and a photograph of our school. Students in New York sent us a photo of themselves and their teacher, among other items.

Within two weeks after the start of our electronic exchanges, all eight participating classrooms began organizing and researching one or more topics related to our common theme, "Global Issues." A teacher from one of the schools in Indiana posted the following message:

> I will have two classes participating in the circle—both of them are Current Affairs classes. We will be working on a problem related to the environment or endangered species. We have begun research and will continue to narrow our idea. I am going to let my students do a great deal of communicating—I think it is more fun for them that way. My 1:30 class will be sending this message. For most of them it is their first experience with tele-

communications. We will be reading and sending mail several times a week—probably reading every day.

The teacher in New York wrote about her plans for her students' "Global Issues" project:

> My students most likely will select the broad idea of "Improving World Relations". . . . Using that broad topic, students will explore various related aspects such as perestroika, nuclear weapons and arms limitations, human rights, the United Nations, tourism, and protecting world peace and environment.

One group of students from the New York school decided to prepare a paper dealing with the Berlin Wall conflict. To gather information for their report, then, they posted a list of questions and asked the students in West Berlin to answer them. Some of the questions included:

1. Do you know any East German escapees?
2. Are your lives at all affected by the situation?
3. Does this topic receive a lot of coverage in the media of your country?

Within a week, the West Berlin students wrote back with responses that included personal anecdotes and other insightful information. A few weeks later, one of the West Berlin students posted another message, one of the most exciting exchanges we received all semester. It began: "Hi, there, from Berlin. I have some important news for you! Communists open Berlin Wall. . . ." The student combined an eyewitness account with a summary of local media coverage to give us an extraordinary report of this historic event. The student ended his report by saying, "I've written this text in very big cooperation with my dictionary."

Another group of students concentrated their efforts on trying to do something about the ozone layer. Here is a message they sent:

> We are concerned with an important issue in our world today. It has been given a lot of thought, but no one has taken any action. The ozone layer is depleting as we speak. If something is not done right now, there will be little hope of saving it for the future. To save the ozone layer, we need everyone's help!!! . . . Some questions that we would like your classes to answer are
>
> 1. How many of you use aerosol products (deodorant, hair spray, etc.)?
> 2. How many of you would be willing to refrain from using these products as a step against the companies that produce them? . . .

Three more questions followed, and the note ended in a plea for a prompt response. Within a few days, almost all of the participating teachers had polled their classes and electronically returned the results of the survey to these students.

Through such exchanges of information, we helped each other investigate various global issues and prepare reports that described our findings and insights. It was a wonderful experience for my students as they wrote for a real audience and made connections with their peers and shared insights and information—all accomplished simply by "talking on the spur of the modem."

International Education and Resource Network (I*EARN)

In January, 1991, I was approached by the administrators at Shorecrest High. It seemed that a coordinator of instructional technology in Israel, Gideon Goldstein, was seeking an electronic partner in the Pacific Northwest to work on a media ecology project with a class of Israeli students. Since I was the school's local "Modem Monster," I was tapped for participation in this project.

I began corresponding electronically with Gideon over the International Education and Resource Network (I*EARN), a network created and sponsored by the Copen Family Fund in New York.[4] The network is part of a larger computer system being run by the Institute for Global Communications, based in San Francisco. In my first electronic note to Gideon, I introduced myself and told him that I would attempt to find a suitable class at Shorecrest High that would be interested in collaborating on the media project. But before we could accomplish much in our planning efforts, we were interrupted by the start of the Persian Gulf War. It appeared that we would have to cancel this project since schools were closed immediately in Israel. But then something else began to happen: Gideon started sending us daily eyewitness, "up close and personal" reports about the war and how it was affecting Israeli citizens. And we heard from several Israeli students, too, who wrote us messages. We heard about one student who was afraid to take a shower because she might miss hearing the alarm that signaled an impending missile attack. We heard from another student, writing late one evening, who said that he was going to bed now and that he hoped there wouldn't be an attack tonight: "It is the worst time to get bombed." My students as well as others around the country followed Gideon's daily narrative reports and asked a million questions. Gideon never failed to respond within twenty-four hours to all inquiries. We generated more than 300 pages of correspondence this way.

There were some humorous moments and messages mixed in with the more serious reports and expressions of personal opinions. An Israeli student wrote one time, asking the American students to suggest a name for the gas mask that he had to carry around with him everywhere: "All the students in my school gave their gas masks a name, but I just can't find a name to give mine. Do you have any ideas?" Sure enough, a class of elementary students in New York wrote back a few days later, saying "We made a list of suggested names for your gas mask. Maybe one will appeal to you." Among their list were such names as "Airhead," "Dark Vader," "Fidel Gastro," "Unleaded Only," and "BUM (Big Ugly Mask)."

Another humorous moment occurred when Kim, one of my students, wrote to Gideon and ended her note by referring to Efrat, an Israeli student who had written earlier: "Please say hello to Efrat for me. . . . I hope to hear from him again." Well, the next morning, there was an electronic letter from Efrat waiting for us when we logged onto the network:

> Guess who . . .
>   Before saying anything, even hello, I must say one thing to Kim and everybody else who might make this same mistake. I'm not a "he," not a "him"! I'm a she, her, a girl, a woman, a female: of the sex that can give birth to children or produce eggs (Oxford Advanced Learner's Dictionary). I'm even a feminist. I never thought anyone could make this mistake because Efrat is a feminine name, and I never heard about a boy named Efrat. But I guess I understand the mistake because you can't find out whether it's a boy or a girl because in English the verbs are the same for the two sexes, not like in Hebrew. O.K. Let's leave this subject and move to other things. . . .

Kim sent a quick reply, apologizing for her mistake, and the two students went on to correspond many more times, becoming good friends.

The instructional possibilities available through telecommunications became even more apparent as a result of a message that one of my students sent to Gideon one time. In his note, the student asked: "I don't fully understand the reasons why the Israelis and the Palestinians are such enemies. Could you give me some insight into this problem? What kind of effect will the current mideast war have on the Israeli-Palestinian conflict?" Gideon wrote back:

> I have been contemplating for over a week what would be the best way to explain to American students the origin of the Israeli-Arab dispute. The full story fills many books. Little fact, mostly interpretations and even a little fiction have been mixed in the story.
>
> I have decided to approach the issue from a different angle. I want you to do some of the work, and we will try to put the puzzle together. I am certain that several U.S. schools have Israelis as well as Arab students. I would always be judged as another biased individual in this escapade. Therefore we will let your fingers (eyes, ears and brain) do the walking. . . .

Gideon then outlined a step-by-step set of directions, a series of tasks that students should complete to help them find answers to the question of the origins of the Israeli-Arab conflict. His first assignment, for example, involved reading parts of the Bible:

> One of the aspects of this dispute is the old 'I was here first' issue. Your first mission is to check available scriptures for the answer to this question. . . .

Four of my students in my precollege writing class asked if they could take Gideon up on his challenge to research the conflict. After checking with the students' parents to obtain their approval, I had the four students stop working on the regular coursework for the class and begin the research according to Gideon's directions. For the next two months, then, Gideon literally became their teacher. The students reported to the library daily instead of coming to my class; they engaged in almost-daily correspondence with Gideon, reporting on their progress and emerging insights, asking questions, and requesting further direction. Gideon instructed the students to make a chart listing each mideast conflict that occurred over the past four decades, to interview a rabbi, to consult maps, and to do further reading—a *lot* of reading. And this instruction was all accomplished electronically. In the end, the students gave an oral presentation of their conclusions to their classmates and sent a written report to Gideon.

Soon after the mideast conflict ended, I was able to arrange things so Gideon could not only visit Seattle, but also come to Shorecrest High to speak to the student body at an all-school assembly, and he even appeared at our open house for parents that evening. The highlight of his visit, of course, was the moment when he met in person the four students with whom he had worked steadily for the past two months. It was an emotional meeting.

Opportunities such as these provided by AT&T's Learning Network and the I*EARN project represent cooperative community efforts, a way of learning that will be characteristic of instruction in the schools for the twenty-first century. Through such telecommunications projects, teachers and students can explore and experience the future of education.

Notes

1. WIER entered its seventh year in 1994 with some eighty schools and fourteen writers. For more information, contact: Writers in Electronic Residence, 24 Ryerson Avenue, Suite 207, Toronto, Ontario, Canada M5T 2P3; telephone: 416-861-2490; facsimile: 416-861-0090; Internet e-mail: wier@cosy.edu.yorku.ca

2. For detailed information about the Learning Network and to obtain an application form, write to: AT&T Learning Network, P.O. Box 6391, Parsippany, NJ 07054; telephone: 1-800-367-7225.

3. The above descriptions of the six curriculum areas are taken from page 3 of the promotional brochure (© 1991) provided by the AT&T Learning Network.

4. Teachers may join the International Education and Resource Network (I*EARN) and enable their students to engage in electronic correspondence with other classrooms around the country and around the world. The I*EARN network sponsors many multicultural and international projects for students and teachers and encourages your participation. To subscribe to the network, write to the following address: Institute for Global Communications, 18 DeBoom Street, San Francisco, CA 94107. To receive additional information about the I*EARN network, write Ed Gragert at the following address: Copen Family Fund, 345 Kear Street, Yorktown Heights, NY 10598; telephone: 1-914-962-5864; Internet e-mail: ed1.igc.apc.org

Author

Jeffrey N. Golub is currently working as assistant professor of English education at the University of South Florida in Tampa. For twenty years, he taught English, speech communication, and writing classes at both the junior high and senior high school levels in Seattle, Washington. In 1990, while teaching at Shorecrest High School in Seattle, he received the State Farm Insurance Company's "Good Neighbor" Award for innovative teaching.

In addition to his teaching, Golub works extensively with the National Council of Teachers of English. He has served on NCTE's Executive Committee, Secondary Section Committee, and the Commission on the English Curriculum. For three years, he was co-editor of the "Junior High/Middle School Idea Factory" column in *English Journal,* and he has edited two books in NCTE's Classroom Practices series, *Activities to Promote Critical Thinking* (1986) and *Focus on Collaborative Learning* (1988). In 1989, he won *English Journal*'s writing award along with Louann Reid, his co-author.

Golub has given several presentations and workshops at NCTE conferences and for teachers and school districts across the country. His topics have included the interactive classroom, computers and writing instruction, and responding to poetry and other literature.

And he loves chocolate.